MASS CULTURE, LANGUAGE AND ARTS IN INDIA

MASS CULTURE LANGUAGE AND ARTS IN INDIA

Papers presented at a Symposium at Duke University, Durham, North Carolina

Edited by
MAHADEV L. APTE

BOMBAY
POPULAR PRAKASHAN

POPULAR PRAKASHAN PRIVATE LIMITED
35 C Tardeo Road, Popular Press Bldg.. Bombay 400 034

© 1978 by Mahadev L. Apte

First published
1978

(3163)

PRINTED IN INDIA
BY MANMOHAN S. BHATKAL AT POPULAR BOOK DEPOT (PRINTING DIVISION)
DR. BHADKAMKAR MARG, BOMBAY 400 007 AND PUBLISHED BY RAMDAS G. BHATKAL
FOR POPULAR PRAKASHAN PVT. LTD., 35C TARDEO ROAD, BOMBAY 400 034

PREFACE

The papers in this volume were prepared for a symposium on "Mass Culture, Language and Arts in India" held at Duke University, Durham, North Carolina, U.S.A., March 13-15, 1970....The symposium was sponsored and supported by the Committee on Comparative Studies in Southern Asia and the Committee on International Studies at Duke University. I am grateful to both these committees for their generous support to the symposium. I should also like to thank all contributors who presented papers at the symposium and participated in various discussions. I am indebted to Judit Apte for her considerable help with the organizing of the symposium. Thanks are also due to Mrs. Marion Salinger, Administrative Assistant to International Programs at Duke University for her assistance in taking care of the administrative details.

The paper "Traditional Forms of Mass Media in Maharashtra" by K. Narain Kale is being published posthumously. Mr. Kale passed away in early 1974.

Although efforts have been made to standardize the transcription of words from Indian languages, because of the considerable variation in the practices followed by different authors, there are likely to be some discrepancies. I hope the readers will kindly overlook them.

MAHADEV APTE

CONTENTS

Preface   v

1. Introduction
   MAHADEV L. APTE   1

2. Mass Culture in Historical and Contemporary India
   JOSEPH W. ELDER   10

3. Language and Mass Communication in India
   FRANKLIN C. SOUTHWORTH   30

4. Forms and Functions of Mass Media — The Press
   KUSUM NAIR   54

5. The Ecology of Art: India and the West
   WALTER M. SPINK   72

6. Music and Mass Culture in India
   MAHADEV L. APTE   98

7. Traditional Forms of Mass Media in Maharashtra
   K. NARAIN KALE   121

8. The Influence of Mass Culture on Folk Culture in a Mysore Village
   HELEN ULLRICH   134

9. Medieval Bengali Culture: The Nonelite Elements
   TAPAN RAYCHAUDHURI   142

10. Sitala and the Art of Printing: The Transmission and Propagation of the Myth of the Goddess of Smallpox in Rural West Bengal
   RALPH W. NICHOLAS   152

11. A Kerala Village Temple Festival: Ritual and Folk Art Forms as Communicators of Traditional Culture
   CLIFFORD R. JONES   181

CONTRIBUTORS

MAHADEV L. APTE is Associate Professor of Anthropology at Duke University. He received his doctorate in Linguistics and Anthropology from the University of Wisconsin at Madison, Wisconsin in 1962. He held previous positions at Poona University (Deccan College), the University of Wisconsin at Madison, and the School of Oriental and African Studies in London. He has done fieldwork in Maharashtra and Tamil Nadu. His professional interests include sociolinguistics, structural linguistics, South Asian societies and cultures, and Marathi language and literature. He has published several articles on sociolinguistics in South Asia and on various aspects of Marathi literature.

JOSEPH W. ELDER is currently Professor of Sociology and South Asian Studies at the University of Wisconsin, Madison, Wisconsin. He received his doctorate from Harvard University. He has conducted research in Tamil Nadu, Uttar Pradesh, and Nepal on such topics as industrialism and Hinduism, attitude changes, patterns of social mobility, the impact of planned development programs, and regional contrasts within India. His major publications include *Lectures in Indian Civilization* and *Chapters in Indian Civilization*.

K. NARAIN KALE was a prominent literary critic in Marathi. He was associated with Marathi film industry in various capacities in the thirties and the forties. He was also connected with Marathi stage and was one of the pioneers of the early experiments. He was the editor of a noted literary magazine. His publications include translations of Sanskrit and English plays, and articles on various aspects of Marathi stage.

CLIFFORD R. JONES is currently Assistant Professor of South Asian Art at the University of Pennsylvania. He received his doctorate from the University of Pennsylvania. He has conducted extensive research in India. His research interests are traditional art and theater forms of India, particularly those involved in living religious ritual, their relationships to canonical texts of the classical and medieval periods, and their function as communication systems of traditional cultural values. His major publications include *Kathakali: An Introduction to the Dance Drama of Kerala* and "Bhagavata Mela Natakam, a Traditional Dance-Drama Form", *Journal of Asian Studies*, XXII, 2.

KUSUM NAIR is currently Visiting Researcher in the Food Institute at the East-West Center in Hawaii. She has worked as correspondent for Indian, European, and American newspapers in the area of economic and political affairs and development. Since 1958 she has been doing serious research and writing in the field of rural development and has held research positions at various universities in the U.S. Her major publications include *Blossoms in the Dust*, *The Lonely Furrow* and *Three Bowls of Rice*.

RALPH W. NICHOLAS is Professor of Anthropology at the University of Chicago. He received his Ph.D. from the University of Chicago. He previously served on the faculties of Michigan State University, Portland State University in Oregon, and the School of Oriental and African Studies in London. His research has been primarily in West Bengal and Bangladesh and has dealt with cultural ecology, rural politics, religious beliefs and practices, and Bengali culture as a symbolic system. He is currently engaged in work on Bengali kinship and in a translation and analysis of the *Sitala Mangal*.

TAPAN RAYCHAUDHURI is Reader in Modern South Asian History at Oxford University and Professorial Fellow at St. Antony's College in Oxford. He was educated at Presidency College, Calcutta, and Balliol College in Oxford and received his D.Phil. from these institutions. He has previously held positions at the National Archives of India, Delhi School of Economics, and Delhi University. His major publications include *Bengal Under Akbar and Jahangir* and *Jan Company in Coromandel, 1605-1690*.

FRANKLIN C. SOUTHWORTH is Associate Professor of South Asian Linguistics at the University of Pennsylvania. He received his doctorate from Yale University. He has done fieldwork in Maharashtra and Tamil Nadu. His research interests are sociolinguistics (synchronic and diachronic), areal linguistics, multilingualism, semantics, and South Asian languages. His publications include *Foundations of Linguistics* (with C. J. Daswani), *Contact and Convergence in South Asian Languages* (with Mahadev L. Apte) and *The Student's Hindi-Urdu Reference Manual*.

WALTER SPINK is currently Professor of the History of Art at the University of Michigan, Ann Arbor, Michigan. He received his Ph.D. from Harvard University. He has previously taught at Brandeis University. His chief research interests are early Buddhist and Hindu art of India. His major publications include *Ajanta to Ellora*, *Krishnamandala*, and *The Axis of Eros*.

HELEN ULLRICH is Associate Professor of Anthropology at the State University of New York, Albany. She received her Ph.D. in Linguistics from the University of Michigan, Ann Arbor, Michigan. She has done fieldwork in Karnataka state in India. Her research interests include South Asian linguistics, sociolinguistics, social and linguistic change, and Dravidian languages. Her publications include "Linguistic Aspects of Antiquity: A Dialect Study," *Anthropological Linguistics* 13(3), and "Morphological Coexistence: A Key to Linguistic Convergence," in Southworth and Apte (eds.) *Contact and Convergence in South Asian Languages*.

MASS CULTURE, LANGUAGE AND ARTS IN INDIA

1

INTRODUCTION

MAHADEV L. APTE

Indian society and culture have intrigued westerners for a long time. There are both scholarly and popular writings that deal with numerous facets of India. However, in this huge mass of literature there does not exist any discussion of the concept of mass culture as it relates to India.

The reason for this lack may be historical. Western scholars did not pay much attention to the concept of mass culture even in the analyses and descriptions of their own societies until the beginning of the twentieth century. With the rapid development of technology, however, there emerged various mass media, especially radio and films. Communication became possible over large geographical areas, affecting multitudes of communities within societies at large, communities which hitherto were primarily engulfed in their own local and/or sub-regional socio-cultural milieu and had minimal contact with other segments of society. The advent of television, which reached into every household bringing live events from afar into homes for the average person not only offered mass entertainment but also began to influence the formation of mass opinion, ideologies, and likes and dislikes. These developments were responsible for drawing the attention of western scholars, primarily social scientists and humanists, to the effect of mass media on society, and to the conceptualization of mass culture as different from elite culture and folk culture.

The purpose behind organizing this symposium was to formalize the concept of mass culture as it is generally understood and is applied to western societies, and to investigate if it could be relevant to the study of Indian society and culture. If it is, what is its nature and to what extent is it related to socio-cultural change now occurring in Indian society. Such an attempt seemed appropriate because conditions favourable to the development of mass culture have been emerging in India with the processes of democratization, industrialization, urbanization and modernization.

The main theme of the symposium was to determine the role of language, mass communication, and art in the development of mass culture since they were felt to be the major tools influencing its creation. These in turn were being affected by such media factors as the developments of the printing press, newspapers, radio and films; the growth in literacy; exposure to new political ideologies; direct participation of the masses in choosing a government; and a resurgence of linguistic and regional identities competing with national identity.

It was also necessary to examine the role of traditional folk arts, religious festivals, and other aspects of folk culture in this changing socio-cultural milieu. In essence then, the focus of the symposium was to define and formulate the concept of mass culture, to present materials related to it, and to analyze the data by answering some of the following questions:

1. How valid is the concept of mass culture in the Indian context both from the synchronic and diachronic viewpoints?

2. What has been and/or could be the role and influence of modern means of communication on the development of mass culture and on the transformation of folk culture? To put it another way, have the localized folk arts such as crafts, dances, folk-music, and folk-lore, often associated with rituals and festivals, been transformed into secular mass arts both in terms of their production and consumption?

3. Did the regional linguistic movements develop standardized communicative codes which, instead of being puristic, rigid, traditional, and literary, would be more representative of the popular colloquial speech styles?

4. Along with the linguistic and regional developments, are there developing some pan-Indian aspects of culture that could be identified with the new image of Indian nationhood?

5. What was the probability of the emergence of a new mass

culture which would be distinct from either the "Great Tradition" or the numerous "Little Traditions"? Would this new culture incorporate some features of the "Great Tradition" by simplifying them so as to be within the grasp of the masses? Would it also assimilate some features of the various "Little Traditions" by changing their local characteristics into pan-Indian features?

6. How deliberate would the whole process of the development of mass culture be, and what would be the reactions of the elites and purists to it?

The organization of papers in this volume is indicative of the theoretical presentation designed to answer the questions raised above, but with one important proviso. The first five papers by Elder, Southworth, Nair, Spink and Apte are general in their perspective since many theoretical issues are discussed in them in the pan-Indian context. On the other hand, the remaining papers by Kale, Ullrich, Raychaudhuri, Nicholas and Jones are more specific in nature because each deals with individual instances illustrating some of the general theoretical points.

The opening paper by Elder sets the theme of the symposium by examining the concept of mass culture in its broadest Indian context. After briefly tracing the history of the concept in the western literature, Elder extricates the following four dimensions from the pioneering essay of Dwight Mcdonald on mass culture: Quality of Art; Expensiveness of Art; Individual Creation vs. Collective Creation; and Target Audience. He states that all these dimensions cannot be applied equally for determining the concept of mass culture; for instance Target Audience is more significant than all others. He then describes four types of culture categories — patron culture, artist culture, folk/community culture, and mass culture — using the criterion of Target Audience. After presenting factual information from Indian history, he hypothesizes that all these culture categories were present in India from ancient times, but at different periods one or the other was prominent. If we accept Elder's definition of mass culture, namely, that it consists of artistic products aimed at the general unrestricted public, then, he claims, that mass culture is as old as society. He argues that there is an historic continuity from the crude mass-produced icons of Harappa to the crude mass-produced icons of today. Elder concedes that with the advances of new technology, mass culture has bloomed hundred-fold, but, he claims, it was there before nonetheless.

In the final part of his paper Elder succinctly describes the major characteristics of mass culture in India and predicts future developments. Many papers in the volume exemplify and support the theoretical statements made by Elder.

The papers by Southworth and Nair are primarily concerned with communication. Southworth deals with many broad aspects of language and Nair with journalism. Southworth concentrates on discussing the major types of linguistic variations and their present and future roles in developing mass culture. He examines the language used in radio, cinema, newspapers, television, literature, and public writings of signs, notices, posters etc., and argues that, those who determine what the standardized forms of regional languages should be, imitate the model of classical English adopted by the westernized bureaucratic elites during the British period. In his opinion such a model is simply inadequate for mass communication because it brings with it puristic attitudes and the desire to enforce literary styles which are not suitable for mass communication since the masses are not literate. Southworth argues that such puristic attitudes prevail even in the use of language in mass media. Thus the important dimension of Target Audience is ignored by the intellectuals and elites who are responsible for governmental policy for developing mass media. The only exception Southworth mentions, with which other contributors agree, is the film industry. There is general agreement that movies in India cater to the masses and the language used in them is informal and colloquial.

Southworth's argument is a convincing one. He warns that as long as classicalized norms are continually supported by the policy-makers and implementors in education and mass media, institutional development of colloquial speech will not occur and the educational processes will be hindered. It should be noted here, that most of the fictional literature in the regional languages *does* seem to adopt popular speech styles. However, because of the low rate of literacy, it is difficult to judge the

Introduction

impact of such literature on mass communication.

Southworth's view that mass media is oblivious to the needs of the Target Audience, namely the masses, is forcefully supported by Nair, an experienced journalist. She contends that the press in India is ineffective in reaching the masses for a variety of reasons. Her arguments for this position are many: those who manage and edit newspapers are urban elites and do not know anything about mass culture; press coverage of rural areas, where eighty per cent of the population lives, is inadequate; thus the rural and urban segments of the population are ignorant of each other; the press is primarily concerned with influencing the government rather than providing information to their readers; and finally, the interpretation of national policies by the newspapers is full of vague rhetoric and total irrelevance.

Although Nair's position appears extreme, she backs up her arguments with statistical data and her own personal experiences during her extensive tours in the rural areas of India. For example, there are more English-language newspapers in the country than those in any one of the major regional languages although English is spoken by less than seven per cent of the population.

Both Southworth and Nair claim that mass media is not really oriented towards the masses, and that whatever development of mass culture occurred has taken place despite the puristic attitudes of language planners and of those incharge of the press and of the government-controlled radio.

The papers by Spink and Apte are devoted to discussing the relationship of art and music to the development of mass media. Spink's paper has a lengthy discussion of western art and its inherent ideology which he compares to Indian art. He argues that until the British arrived, Indian art was essentially a variation on, and elaboration of the basic themes imbibed in Hinduism. Thus there was considerable resistance to change, and if any change did occur, it was through augmentation rather than negation or criticism. In this respect, Spink contends, Indian art was very different from western art. Indian art, just as philosophy and world-view, was very much in consonance with nature and did not reflect the kind of struggle between conquering the universe and being controlled by it that western civilization underwent.

With the arrival of the British and the importation of western art and western technological mass media, Spink feels that western art will erode the traditions of Indian imagery. He thinks that traditional folk art is losing its religious significance and is becoming what he calls popular poster art, separating in the process from the cultural context. The potency of the image is being sacrificed for profits by its distribution on a large scale. Thus, Spink seems to agree with Elder that popular mass-produced icons are truly symbols of mass culture and at least for Spink, they are devoid of their traditional and religious associations.

The situation is not much different for music. Apte states that in the pre-modern period, music in India, especially classical music, was exclusively the domain of the elites, while folk music existed independently, and like most of the folk/community culture was very much part of the religious tradition. With the advent of modernization, Indian classical music no longer remains the exclusive domain of a select few, but is being popularized in two ways. First, more people learn it because of the adoption of modern teaching methods which dissolved the earlier one-to-one teacher-disciple relationship and added the notation system so much looked down on by musicians of the previous generations. Secondly, more people listen to classical music, because of its popularization through the radio which has appeal to urban masses.

At the same time, a new kind of music, not of the indigenous genre, but a strange mixture of east and west, began to appear in films. This film music has already encroached on the domains of both classical and folk music. Apte claims that this is the true "popular" music of India catering primarily to the masses.

Despite the somewhat pessimistic outlook of many participants in the symposium concerning the demise of folk culture, attention has been drawn by some contributors to the deliberate efforts by both the central and state governments to revitalize various aspects of folk culture, especially the arts, crafts, music, and folk literature. The emphasis in such revival

Introduction

however, seems to be economic, with an eye on earning valuable foreign exchange by exporting such indigenously produced goods, or by stocking the stores which cater primarily to tourists, and to the Indian elites who have cultivated a liking for folk art.

The remaining papers in this volume provide substantive data by describing specific instances and thus help to illustrate answers in response to the various questions raised earlier.

Kale, for example, describes in detail the various traditional India in the region of Maharashtra and demostrates how they are being transformed from their religious forms to suit the demands of modern times. Many of Kale's arguments are similar to those of Elder, with the addition that in Kale's opinion the fusion of social and religious elements — and their modernization for the masses as demonstrated in a temple festival — is the result of deliberate and conscious planning.

Ullrich discusses the transformation of the traditional folk art in Mysore — the Yakshagana performances — into mass culture with the help of modern technological mass media. She emphasizes how mass culture has gradually intruded into even rural areas and thus co-exists with folk art. Ullrich, like others, suggests that mass culture in India is one of tolerance, stressing the peaceful coexistence of different life-styles.

Raychaudhuri's paper is somewhat different from the rest because it is restricted to explaining the affinities and continuities of the contemporary non-elite culture in Bengal to its counterpart in medieval Bengal. His major hypothesis is that medieval non-elite Bengali culture was a counterpart of modern mass culture, and the apparently parochial nature of this medieval culture was partly due to the limitations of media communication. He argues that medieval Bengali literature, which was largely religious in nature, served the same function as modern mass media with the exception that the time period required for its spread among the masses was considerably longer. But it did help in creating homogeniety of myths and other religious ideas among the masses.

The paper by Nicholas seems to support Raychaudhuri's conclusion by presenting a detailed analysis of the transmission and propagation of the myth of the small-pox goddess in rural

Bengal. The emphasis here is on the processes by which myths are communicated from one generation to the next, and on how they are reinforced in the minds of most members of society. Nicholas stresses the fact that printing has been very influential in the propagation and transmission of this particular myth. In addition, such technology has also aided in standardizing the myth and in spreading the folk culture. The major part of Nicholas's paper is a detailed ethnographic description of the actual performance which he claims is similar to the pre-modern techniques of spreading and retaining various aspects of folk culture. Nicholas' view is similar to that of Elder that mass culture borrows and standardizes elements from folk/community culture.

The final paper by Jones is another example of the transformation of religion-oriented folk culture to mass culture because of modernization. Jones describes vividly a temple festival in a Kerala village and its socio-cultural implication in terms of the participation of different castes in it, the actual ritual that takes place, the procession which is the major part of the festival, and the typically local forms of entertainment connected with it. Like Nicholas, Jones presents detailed ethnographic data. There is an interesting similarity in Nicholas' and Jones' papers, namely, that the festivals and performances are connected with the goddess of small-pox although they occur in geographically distant parts of India. Jones' concluding remarks point out how this traditionally religious folk festival has been elevated to a mass level by the process of modernization whereby the impact of the festival has spread not only to all social strata, but also over a wider geographic area. Thus, this too, is another example of the transformation of folk culture into mass culture of modern times.

Despite the wide range of topics discussed in various papers presented in this volume, there are some major gaps. For example, there is very little discussion of contemporary literature in various regional languages and its role in the development of mass culture. Also lacking is some analysis of the popular theatre as it has been emerging in most regions of India, especially among the urban masses.

The analysis and views presented in the papers lead us to

Introduction

the following conclusions concerning the concept of mass culture, its relevance to contemporary India, and its relation to language and arts.

1. The process of modernization in India has signalled the development of mass culture, primarily because of the impact of modern mass media which have brought with them a variety of western modes of expressions. This development of mass culture is further accelerated by the introduction of new technology which makes it possible for artifacts to be mass-produced and mass-distributed.

2. The folk culture and traditions are being gradually replaced by the advancing mass media techniques because there seems to be a continuous transformation of such folk culture from its religious orientation to a more secular one. And although in some cases the existing folk art forms seem to benefit from the new mass media in reaching larger audiences, their standardization in this process has converted them from folk-culture to mass culture.

3. Among the modern mass media, movies seem to be the single most powerful force in the formation of mass culture. The popularity and tremendous appeal of films and film music to the majority of Indians is a prime example of this phenomenon. Movies are also responsible for the development of popular colloquial speech styles, and popular fashions.

4. There is still a strong tendency on the part of those who are responsible for language planning to retain the high puristic attitudes. This hinders the development of standardized communicative codes by using colloquial speech styles and it also hinders the mass education process.

5. The conventional dichotomy of Great *vs.* Little Traditions used by social scientists in the analysis of Indian society and culture is inadequate to describe the phenomenon of the development of mass culture. Although there is some historical continuity between the contemporary mass culture and the pre-modern folk or non-elite culture, the nature of the emerging mass culture clearly indicates that it is an admixture not only of the indigenous high and folk culture, but also of western culture.

2

MASS CULTURE IN HISTORICAL AND CONTEMPORARY INDIA

JOSEPH W. ELDER

I. MASS CULTURE: SOME WESTERN DEFINITIONS AND HYPOTHESES

Before one can systematically discuss a topic like mass culture in India, one needs to turn at least briefly to the question: What *is* mass culture? How has it been defined outside India? Is this definition applicable inside India? What other types of culture are there from which the concept of mass culture should be kept analytically distinct? And what is known about mass culture in other parts of the world that might have relevance for mass culture in India?

The Frenchman, Alexis de Tocqueville, was a pioneer writer on what has come to be called mass culture. Commenting on his observations in the United States in the 1830's, de Tocqueville wrote:

> In aristocratic ages, the object of the arts is…to manufacture as well as possible…the handicraftsmen work for only a limited number of fastidious customers…(In) democracies there is always a multitude of persons whose wants are above their means, and who are very willing to take up with imperfect satisfaction rather than abandon the object of their desires altogether. The artisan readily understands these passions…he strives to invent methods which may enable him not only to work better, but cheaper and quicker; or, if he cannot succeed in that, to diminish the intrinsic quality of the thing he makes, without rendering it wholly unfit for

the use for which it is intended. Thus the democratic principle ... induces the artisan to produce with great rapidity many imperfect commodities, and the consumer to content himself with those commodities.[1]

De Tocqueville's view that the wider the circle of art consumers the lower the quality of art produced struck a resonant — even sinister — chord among certain western historians and the art critics. In 1918 the German historian, Oswald Spengler, in his *Decline of the West*, identified "mass art" as one of the symptoms that a High Culture had reached its crest and was irrevocably sinking into its dying stage.

In 1929 the Spanish philosopher, Jose Ortega Y Gasset, in *The Revolt of the Masses*, wrote:

The characteristic of the hour is that the commonplace mind, knowing itself to be commonplace, has the assurance to proclaim the rights of the commonplace and to impose them wherever it will...The mass crushes beneath it everything that is different, everything that is excellent, individual, qualified and select.[2]

In his multi-volume *A Study of History*, published between 1939 and 1961, the English historian Arnold Toynbee, like Oswald Spengler, saw the irreversible vulgarization of morals, arts, and institutions as one of the clear symptoms of a dying civilization.

Perhaps one of the best-known writers on the concept of mass culture has been the American editor, publisher, and critic, Dwight Macdonald. In his 1953 essay entitled "A Theory of Mass Culture,"[3] Dwight Macdonald introduced and defined a set of terms that have subsequently been often used in discussions of mass culture. Macdonald distinguishes between three basically different forms of art: "High Culture," "Folk Art," and "Mass Culture."

"High Culture," as Macdonald sees it, includes those artistic

1. Alexis de Tocqueville, *Democracy in America*, New York: Vintage Books 1958, Vol. II, pp. 50-52.
2. Jose Ortega Y Gasset, *The Revolt of the Masses*, New York: W.W. Norton, 1957, p. 18.
3. *Diogenes*, No. 3 (Summer, 1953), pp. 1-17.

achievements traditionally recorded by historians — the temples, castles, and cathedrals, and the musical, literary, and artistic masterpieces. "High Culture" is designed for the *cognoscenti*, the upperclass, the elite, the urban, and the urbane. "High Culture" is quality art, the art that puts the stamp of genius on an age, the art from which future generations draw inspiration.

"Folk Art" is a completely different genre. It is the spontaneous expression of the people sharing "common interests, work, traditions, values, and sentiments." It is authentic, shaped by the people themselves satisfying their own needs, contributing to their "private little garden walled off from the great formal park of their masters' High Culture." Robert Burns, Charlie Chaplin, and Sholem Aleichem would be western examples of folk artists.

"Mass Culture" is still a different form of artistic production. "Mass Culture" is to "High Culture" what cancer is to healthy tissue or what a caterpillar is to a leaf. "Mass Culture" feeds on "High Culture," debasing "High Culture" and putting nothing back. It is "very, very democratic; it absolutely refuses to discriminate against, or between, anything or anybody." It mixes all together, destroying values, since value judgments require discrimination. "Mass Culture" is manufactured collectively by production-line specialists, coordinating, fitting to tested formulas, packaging, and marketing. No single brain is in command; no single artist sees the work as his own. The team of specialists is hired by businessmen to exploit consumers. The consumers are reduced to passive participants, choosing whether or not to buy the "Mass Culture" product. Macdonald concludes:

> The Lords of *kitsch* [a German term for "Mass Culture"] sell culture to the masses. It is a debased, trivial culture that voids both the deep realities (sex, death, failure, tragedy) and also the simple, spontaneous pleasures ... The masses, debauched by several generations of this sort of thing, in turn come to demand trivial and comfortable cultural products. Which came first .... the mass demand or its satisfaction (and further stimulation) is a question as academic as it is unanswerable.[4]

4. Ibid., pp. 15-16.

Drawing on his definitions of "High Culture," "Folk Art" and "Mass Culture," Macdonald sets forth a number of propositions summarizing what "Mass Culture" has done in the United States and suggesting what "Mass Culture" may do anywhere else it appears:

1. "Mass Culture" destroys "High Culture". With the disappearance of cultural elites, "High Culture" must compete for survival in the public market place. And in the public market place "Mass Culture" has all the advantages: it is more easily understood and enjoyed by the consumers; its products heavily outnumber "High Culture's" products; and it can consistently undersell "High Culture."

2. Where "Mass Culture" does not destroy "High Culture," it corrupts it. "Mass Culture" is quick to seize anything new, standardize it, and mass produce it. The end product is a homogenization of "High" and "Mass Culture." Macdonald notes: "There is slowly emerging a tepid, flaccid Middlebrow Culture that threatens to engulf everything in its spreading ooze... There is nothing more vulgar than sophisticated *kitsch*."

3. "Mass Culture" also destroys "Folk Art." Aiming at majority tastes, "Mass Culture" either bypasses unique traditions and cultural idioms or it blends them into a homogenized totality. According to Macdonald, "... the Folk artist today lacks the cultural roots and intellectual toughness...to resist for long the pressures of Mass Culture. His taste can easily be corrupted, his sense of his own special talent and limitations [can easily be] obscured..." The chance for a Folk artist to modify his product and attain "Mass Culture" stardom will prove too much for most, if not all, of the Folk artists. Witness the decline of Walt Disney from the creator of the lively and original Mickey Mouse to the manager of the extended plastic and papier-mâché amusement park empire called Disneyland.

II. STEPS TOWARD CONCEPTUAL CLARIFICATION

An examination of Dwight Macdonald's concepts of "High Culture," "Folk Art," and "Mass Culture" reveals that he has incorporated several separate dimensions in his categories. If these dimensions always appear, increase, decrease, and disappear together, something can be said for retaining a multidimensional concept. If the dimensions do not coalesce, it may be useful to isolate the component parts and decide which single dimension offers the most fruitful handle for analysis. At least four different dimensions can be identified within Macdonald's composite categories.

A. *A Quality-of-Art Dimension*

This refers to the intrinsic aesthetic merit of the production, be it music, dance, drama, literature, painting, or sculpture. Macdonald renders judgment on artistic quality, whatever the medium; that it may be "High Culture," "Folk Art," or "Mass Culture," is irrelevant. Thus, according to Macdonald, the poet Rimbaud, the mystery writer Conan Doyle, the novelist James Joyce, the composer Stravinsky, and the painter Picasso have all produced genuine, quality "High Culture." The poet Stephen Phillips, the novelist Somerset Maugham, the composer Sir Edward Elgar, and the painter Rockwell Kent have produced only spurious "High Culture" — something which may pass for the real thing but isn't.

When one recognizes that certain artists whom Macdonald praises others deplore, that artists or musicians regarded highly in the twenties are ignored in the seventies, that a novel or poem thought refreshing and original today may seem corny in another decade, one recognizes how uncertain a dimension this is. This is not to suggest there is no difference between "good" and "bad" art — only that the criteria change from person to person and from time to time — and certainly from society to society. If one is trying to sort a phenomenon into analytically-useful categories, the Quality-of-Art dimension poses difficulties.

B. *An Expensiveness-of-Art Dimension*

Implicit in the writings of men from de Tocqueville to Macdonald is the view that quality art is expensive and can only be afforded by the upper classes, while tasteless imitations are inexpensive and hence can be consumed by the lower classes. This expensive-inexpensive distinction has the virtue of being relatively amenable to measurement. However, even here the standards can be highly variable. How often has a masterpiece been sold for a few coins by a hungry artist, only to become a multi-thousand dollar treasure years later after the artist has been "discovered"? Or how often has an expensive painting — thought to be the work of a great master — been declared valueless when it is shown that a fraud, someone other than the great master, painted it — even though there has been no change in the intrinsic quality of the painting before and after the fraud's discovery? One of the most expensive art forms to produce is the cinema spectacular. But there are few who would argue that this therefore makes it the most valuable art form. The market value of an art product is subject to changing whims, tastes, and scarcities — elements that have little to do with innate artistic quality.

Any assumptions that the wealthy consume good art while the poor consume bad must come to terms with such negative cases as the tasteless expenditures of Thorstein Veblon's leisure class in America, the inflated panegyric of Sanskrit court poetry, and the heavy-handed flattery of Abu'L Fazl's Akbar-namah.

C. The Individual-Creation vs. Collective-Creation Dimension

Certain art is produced by the individual artist — alone with an instrument or working with his paints, in his garret, at his desk, in his humble cottage, or communing with nature. Other art is the product of collaboration, specialization, and the division of labor. Macdonald suggests that the individual art product is, in most instances, superior to the collaborative art product. According to Macdonald "Unity is essential in art: it cannot be achieved by a production line of specialists, however competent." Nonetheless, the cathedrals of Notre Dame and Chartres, the *stupas* and gates at Sanchi, the paintings and sculpturing at Ellora and Ajanta, even some of the miniature paintings from the Mughul courts are the products of many hands. Certain types of music, dance presentations, and dramatic performances are corporate efforts. Much of the classical literature, both East and West, is the work of many different authors — the Bible, possibly the *Iliad*, Greek and Roman myths, the Jataka tales, and the Puranas. Even when one can attribute the name of a poet to one particular version of the *Ramayana* or *Mahabharata*, be it Vyasa, Valmiki, Tulsidas, or Kamban, one is left with the question: to what extent is this version the creation of a single artist, and to what extent is the artist merely the summarizer and compiler, not the creator? In view of how difficult it often is to draw clear lines between individual creations and collective creations, this dimension, too, seems of limited usefulness in discussing Mass Culture.

D. *A Target Audience Dimension*

Of all the dimensions Macdonald incorporates in his "High Culture," "Folk Art," and "Mass Culture" distinctions, the one that seems both easiest to apply and the most suggestive of hypotheses is the target audience dimension. This dimension asks: "To whom does the artist direct his art?" Macdonald identifies three types of audiences: (1) the *cognoscenti* or refined elite for "High Culture," (2) the "folk" for "Folk Art," and (3) the masses for "Mass Culture."

Upon closer view, it is apparent that Macdonald includes two different types of audience in his *cognoscenti*, (1) the patrons who support the artist financially, and (2) other artists or the artistic community. An artist may perform sufficiently differently before these two audiences to warrant dealing with them separately.

In the following chart, I have focussed on the single dimension of "Target Audience" rather than on Macdonald's composite dimensions of "High Culture," "Folk Art," and "Mass Culture." I have also divided the *cognoscenti* into Patron Audiences and Artist audiences.

Organising defining characteristics into a chart like the following one helps underscore a number of points: (1) In the "Target Audience" dimension, three of the four audiences are restricted — the Patrons, the Artists, and the Folk or Community. In each case, the artist directs his art at a defined segment of the population — not the total population. The fourth audience, the unrestricted one, is the Public. This is the audience to which Mass Culture is directed. The unrestricted nature of

Target Audience	Type of Culture	Performer's Support	Performer's Training
Patron audience (restricted) courts, temples, wealthy persons.	Patron Culture	Patronage: individual or collective, direct or indirect.	Training by specialists in codified aesthetic canons.
Artist audience (restricted)	Artist Culture	Unsystematic support: payment for instruction, remission of instruction costs.	Training by specialists in codified aesthetic canons.
Folk or Community audience (restricted)	Folk/Community Culture	Unsystematic support: contributions, maintenance, or no support.	Self-instruction or training by other folk/community performers.
Public audience (unrestricted)	Mass Culture	The "Market" reimbursement for services, employee wages in agencies manipulation the market.	Training by specialists in codified aesthetic canons, self-instruction, training by specialists in Mass Culture.

the audience may help account for important differences between Mass Culture and the other three forms of Culture.

(2) Only two of the four audiences systematically provide financial support for the artist; these two are the Patrons and the Public. The other two audiences (Artist, and Folk or Community) rarely provide an artist with a secure source of income.

(3) Different target audiences expect different types of training of their performers. Patrons and artists typically insist that those performing for them be trained according to some codified and respected aesthetic canons. This may require years of training and apprenticing. Folk or Community audiences, on the other hand, expect a self-made performer, or at most a performer who has apprenticed with some other local performer. These audiences want a performer who has captured their idiom in his music, painting, writing, or action — a performer who is unconventional because he has never learned the standard conventions, a performer with a limited appeal because he has chosen a limited audience to which to appeal. The Public, the consumer of Mass Culture, calls on performers of all kinds, trained as well as selftaught by other folk/community performers. In time, those involved in Mass Culture can even begin to establish their own types of training programs and apprenticeships — for commercial artists, film-makers, script writers, cartoonists, composers and arrangers, and a host of others. Such institutions turn out artists not vulgarized by Mass Culture but trained to produce Mass Culture. They have learned the formulas that were successful in the past. They have learned how to analyze public response. They have learned how to shape public tastes. And they are prepared to give the public "what it wants in sizes and shapes to suit every pocketbook."

III. THE APPLICATION OF THE FOUR-CULTURE CATEGORIES TO INDIA

Patron Culture

Much of the art that has survived from Classical and Medieval India is clearly the product of Patron Culture. The

Asoka pillar, combining Achaemenian with Greek artistic traditions, was almost certainly produced by artists in the pay of the Mauryan court. The *stupas* and railings at Bharhut, Buddha Gaya, and Sanchi, the buddha and bodhisattva images in Gandhara and Mathura were almost surely sponsored and paid for by Buddhist monastic or lay organizations. Kalidasa and Sanskrit drama and belles-letters flourished during the Gupta period thanks to the patronage and support they received from the court. The cave temples, sculptures, and paintings at Ajanta, Ellora, and Elephanta were almost certainly created by artists supported by Buddhist, Jain, and Hindu organizations and funded by contributions from the laity. In each of these cases, one may assume that the final art product represented a combination of what the patron wanted and what the artist was willing or able to provide.

During the medieval period, numerous aristocratic and wealthy families patronized the arts. The rajas and gentry of Kerala supported Kathakali dancers and dance troupes. The Muslim Bahmani sultanates in the Deccan financed impressive architectural works. The Hindu Vijayanagara court under Krishna Deva Raya became a literary center, with the eight "elephants" (eight Telugu poets), a flourishing circle of Sanskrit, Tamil and Kannada writers, and a group of dancers developing Bharata Natyam. With temple-building a fashion, even ordinary *nayakas* (provincial viceroys) supported artists and architects to build temples. In North India the court of Akbar and the subsequent Mughuls became distinguished centers of artistic activity, supporting musicians such as Tan Sen, poets like Raja Birbal, painters like Mansur, and scores of masons, inlayers, and architects to build such magnificent monuments as the Moti Masjid within the Red Fort in Delhi, and the royal city at Fathepur Sikri. The Delhi capital became the center of Kathak dance, as did lesser courts in Lahore, Lucknow, Jaipur, Udaipur, and Banaras.

The dependence of artists on their patrons was dramatized when Aurangzeb ascended the Mughul throne. His sharp curtailment of court patronage for music and painting brought an end to an era of artistic productivity. Some of the disbanded artists migrated to Rajasthan, found sponsorship in the

Hindu courts, and developed the Rajput school of painting. Others who found support in some of the small Hindu states in the Punjab hills developed the so called Pahari and Kangra painting style.

Looking at Patron Culture through Indian history, one notes not-to-surprising association between patrons investing money in the arts and the flourishing of those arts. One also notes the different degrees of vulnerability of different types of art forms. Most vulnerable are those, like architecture, that require heavy expenditures of capital and time. Of somewhat intermediate vulnerability are paintings, music, and dance, which sometimes manage to survive in the back rooms of artistic families until such times as sponsorship again becomes available. Least vulnerable seems to be literature. Certain forms of literature appear to flourish in courts. But certain other forms develop far from any court, with little financial support, and no need to please the ears of a wealthy patron.

Artist Culture

Periodically through Indian history, groups of artists have found themselves working in proximity to each other — innovating, modifying, criticizing their own and each others' works, performing essentially for each other rather than for their patrons. The Gupta court of Chandra Gupta II, the Vijayanagara court of Krishna Deva Raya, and the Mughul courts of the emperors Akbar, Jahangir, and Shah Jahan all brought together in one place a "critical mass" of architects, painters, sculptors, poets, and musicians who stimulated each other and who together evolved a distinctive style of art that bore the stamp of that dynasty and era. A patron can buy, but it is the artist who creates, and an artist performing before other artists often finds his creativity enhanced.

To bring together enough artists to generate an Artist Culture can be expensive; hence the frequent relationship between affluence of patronage and emergence of Artist Culture. However, Indian history also contains examples of Artist Cultures arising with a minimum of financial outlay. The semi-mythical early Tamil *sangams* were purported to be convocations of poets (some human, others divine) who gathered in Madurai to listen to each others' works. Those gatherings are not linked even in legend to particular kings or courts. During the last four centuries the Urdu *musha'arah* has become a similar gathering, where poets of varying talent gather to perform for praise, and encourage one another. And today in Tamil Nadu, Karnataka musicians and lovers of Karnataka music still periodically convene from the far corners of India to perform for and listen to each other.

Perhaps the most persistent Artist Cultures in India have been those retained and transmitted through artistic families and lineages. For example, many of the descendents of the famous "Tanjore Quartet" (Chinnaya, Ponnaiah, Vadivelu, and Shivananda Nattuvanar) who did so much to reform Bharata Natyam dance in the early nineteenth century are still active Bharata Natyam dancers and instructors. One such descendent, Kandappa, tutored Bala Saraswati. Their lineage is associated with the village of Pandanallur. Other similar Bharata Natyam lineages are associated with the villages of Tiruvidamaruthur and Vazhuvar. Certain members of the present generation of these lineages have migrated to cities like Madras, Bangalore, and Bombay, where they can draw upon a larger clientele of Bharata Natyam students and supporters. In North India, the continuation and development of the Kathak dance is associated with particular households in Lucknow, Jaipur, and Banaras.

More recently, artists themselves have taken the initiative in founding institutes and academies for the revival of classical arts and experimentation with new forms. Perhaps the best-known center is Rabindranath Tagore's Shantiniketan, founded in 1921. This center played an important part in rediscovering Manipuri dance as well as in encouraging self-consciously *Indian* creative arts. During this same period a somewhat similar institution was founded in Kerala by the poet Vallathol Narayana Menon. Various Kerala dance-drama forms had suffered neglect following the death of such great patrons as Uthram Thirunal, the Maharaja of Travancore (1847-1860). In the 1920's Vallathol organised a lottery, collected Rs. 75,000, and established the Kerala Kala Mandalam. The purpose of the Kala Mandalam was to revitalize the Kathakali, Mohini Attam, and Ottan Thullal dance forms. Vallathol brought together masters of these dance forms, sought additional funds, and eventually organized money-making tours by a Kathakali dance troupe to keep the project solvent.

In the 1950's following Independence, the Indian government founded three national academies for creative arts, the Sangeet Natak Akademi (National Academy of Dance, Drama, and Music), the Sahitya Akademi (National Academy of Letters), and the Lalit Kala Akademi (National Academy of Art), as well as numerous state academies. It remains to be seen to what extent these efforts will succeed in establishing new bases for Artist Cultures.

Folk/Community Culture

"Folk Art," as Macdonald defines it, is art shaped by the people for their own needs. Because of its humble origins and its restricted "community" audience, such art has a degree of spontaneity and authenticity often missing in the more formal art forms. India is full of Folk/Community Culture. Ultimately the *Mahabharata, Ramayana,* the Jataka tales, and the Puranas are products of a Folk Culture. To be sure, some person or persons shaped and edited them into the forms we now know them. But their roots go back to local regions, local heroes, and local bards recounting tales in the vernacular and idiom local people would understand. Regarding the *Mahabharata* and *Ramayana,* even Vyasa and Valmiki, the personages credited with shaping the final Sanskrit forms are seen as sages and holy men — not professional artists.

Much of India's bhakti (devotional) and panthic ("path") poetry falls within the category of Folk/Community Culture. The fact that so many of these devotional poets chose to compose in their own vernaculars rather than in Sanskrit says something about the poets' origins as well as their intended audiences. The Tamil Vaishnavite *alvars* and Shaivite *nayanars* sang hymns of God's praises to the Tamil people in the villages through which they walked. Caitanya's popularisation of Bengali hymn singing, Surdas' and Mirabai's Hindi poems calling Krishna the divine conjugal lover, and Kabir's verses asserting the oneness of God were all directed to particular audiences sharing convictions about the nature of God and man's relationship to Him. The *kirtan,* or public singing of God's name, was often the occasion for presenting new bhakti poetry and hymns. In *kirtans* today one still finds spontaneous performances by folk artists. In Moradabad district in U.P., for example, I recall an old man who attended virtually every accessible *kirtan.* At some point in the proceedings, he would present a special song and dance he had created describing the baby Krishna stealing the ghee. The appearance of a corpus of Mahar neo-Buddhist hymns and poems, many concerning the late Dr. Ambedkar, underscores the liveliness of Folk/Community Culture even today.

Other forms of folk artists still abound in contemporary India. Performing troupes *(Bhanas)* typically including male actors, dancers, musicians, and buffoons (and sometimes also transvestites and women) move from village to village at certain times of the year, entertaining the villagers in their own idiom. A *bhana's* repertoires typically encompasses romantic songs, skits on contemporary topics, political satire, and jokes with local reference. Other folk artists include travelling bards, geneologists, and poets; puppeteers, groups of acrobats, jugglers, firewalkers; and magicians and miscellaneous palmists, fortune tellers, animal trainers, snake charmers, etc. Folk artists are especially in demand at local fairs and festivals, or at times of weddings, the birth of sons, etc., when a wealthy villager may contract with them for a performance, and they in turn are free to receive donations from the spectators. Most of the art they produce will never emerge from the confines of the mud-walled *mohallas* within which the folk artists perform. But such has been the case with all but the most exceptional folk art since time immemorial.

Mass Culture

Mass Culture, as we are defining it, consists of artistic products aimed at the general, unrestricted public. According to this definition, Mass Culture is almost as old as organized society. The figurines of goddesses and the *linga* dug up in Harappa suggest that someone was "cranking out" these products in the probably expressed belief that "no home should be without one." The very textiles that attracted European merchants to India were — many of them — manufactured for a general market with an eye toward what would sell quickly and profitably. For centuries castes of glass and metal bangle-makers have produced multiple copies of standardized bangles, since they have discovered these will sell.

Bernard Rosenbergh may be exaggerating when he states: "If one can hazard a single positive formulation (in the form of a hypothesis) it would be that modern technology is the necessary and sufficient cause of mass culture."[5] Admittedly, however, Mass Culture has bloomed a hundredfold by the advent of machine technology, mass production, and the mass media.

Illiteracy has hampered the growth of printed mass media in India. Nevertheless, India has a sizeable world of publishers and newsprint. In 1967 India listed 8,669 journals, ranging from weeklies to annuals, with a total circulation of over 15.2 million.[6] English-language periodicals enjoyed the largest circulation (3.8 million), followed by Hindi periodicals (3.2 million) and Tamil periodicals (1.7 million). Many of these periodicals can be bought for a few naiya paisa at bookstalls and railroad stations throughout India. Journals often bring out special Diwali issues, running as many as 1,000 pages with special art work and feature-length stories. Such journals have helped contribute to the literary renaissance underway in many of India's languages today. In hundreds of cities and towns magazine-clubs have been organized, centering in reading rooms and depending on participants' dues to finance subscriptions. As literacy increases, one can expect an even more rapid growth in journals of all sorts.

Radios are becoming increasingly popular in India, despite

---

5. Bernard Rosenberg and David M. White (eds.), *Mass Culture: The Popular Arts in America*, Glencoe, III: Free Press, 1960, p. 12. Rosenberg's statement does not take account of evidence that large-scale religious and civil bureaucracies, such as existed in medieval Europe or China, also served as self-conscious bases for the spread of mass culture. Artists' groups, cooperating with the bureaucracies, prepared and disseminated products (e.g., religious pageants) aimed at the general, unrestricted public.

6. These and subsequent figures come from K. E. Eapen, "Development and Reach of Mass Media in India," Chapter VI in Joseph W. Elder (ed.), *Chapters in Indian Civilization*, Debuque: Kendall, Hunt, 1970.

their relatively high cost and licensing requirements. It is estimated that today there are about 8.5 million licensed radios in India and about 1.5 million unlicensed sets. All India Radio now broadcasts over 200,000 hours of programs to areas containing three-fourths of India's population. India is manufacturing her own radios at the rate of about 750,000 sets a year. Television has yet to graduate beyond the experimental stage; there may be as many as 5,500 TV sets owned largely by wealthy urban families. But even in the largest cities, TV programmes are transmitted only a few hours a day. When television achieves a breakthrough in India, one can expect it to have a major impact on the Indian public.

If any of the media have served as pace-setters in Mass Culture, it has been the cinema. Requiring no knowledge of reading and writing and as little as 25 naiya paisa for admission, cinema attendance has become virtually ubiquitous. Some 5,500 movie theaters are scattered over India, ranging from air-conditioned plaster palaces in Delhi and Bombay to temporary tents of palmyra-mat structures propped up in harvested fields in Tamil Nadu. Attendance figures run at about 1.5 billion per year — or approximately 3 film viewings per person per year. The prolificness of the Indian film industry is reflected in the fact that in 1969 India produced the second largest number of feature films of any country in the world (316, contrasted with Japan's top 719 and the U.S. sixth place 168).

With the cinema have come new concepts of speech, dress, lifestyle, values, family relationships, dance and music. What usually appears on the screen is an amalgam of plot sequences drawn from other films, dance routines elaborately costumed and choreographed, and songs galore, accompanied by orchestras of Indian classical and Western jazz instruments, playing melodies from Vienna, Broadway, and Rio de Janeiro, embellished with Karnataka trills and grace notes and undergirded with Indian drumming.

This same sort of music is available from gaudy, uniformed bands that will play for hire at weddings, funerals, or other events. Similar music also fills the air waves; 45 per cent of All India Radio's program hours consist of Indian music, much of it taken from the films. Where the radio leaves off, records and loudspeakers begin, making certain the melodies are heard throughout the land.

What the cinema, radio, and phonograph have done for music, the printing press has done for art. The typical hut, tea-stall, living-room, or store are decorated with brightly-colored pictures. Exchanged annually as gift calendars, or purchased from stationery stores or picture-supply stalls, these pictures depict gatherings of the gods, or single Gods in characteristic poses, devoted worshippers, dramatic moments from the epics or Puranas, blissful cows, holy men, national heroes such as Gandhi or Nehru, notable buildings such as the Red Fort or Taj Mahal, or scenes of chubby children playing with toys. They may even reproduce panels from the Ajanta paintings or sculpture such as the Trimurti in the Elephanta cave.

And at least in certain parts of India, this age of Mass Culture has made it possible for icons to be mass produced and sold. Painted ceramic, wooden, or brass-like metal figures of Ganesh, Hanuman, Krishna, and Lakshmi can be bought at minimum cost to decorate the domestic shrine or mantle. There is historic continuity from the crude, mass-produced icons of Harappa to the crude, mass-produced icons of today.

This paper has tried to sort India's art products into meaningful categories in order to sharpen distinctions between what we shall and shall not call Mass Culture. The last portion of this paper will set forth some tentative propositions regarding Mass Culture in India, if only to focus the problems of data-gathering and data-assessing.

IV. SOME PROPOSITIONS REGARDING MASS CULTURE IN INDIA

1. Mass Culture in India borrows from international (primarily European and American) Mass Culture. Many Mass Culture products are readily imitated and have cross-cultural appeal. People in India exposed to the mass media will share more in the international Mass Culture than will those not exposed to the media.

2. In India, Mass Culture contributes to the sharing of common legends, common representations of deities, common popular songs, common mass media heroes, common styles of clothing, and common speech patterns. People exposed to the mass media will share more of a common culture with others exposed to the media than with others not so exposed.
3. In India, with its major language divisions, most people experience two types of Mass Culture — an all-India culture and a language-specific culture. At certain points the language-specific culture will self-consciously be at variance with the all-India culture, asserting its superiority at the expense of the all-India culture.
4. The all-India Mass Culture is one of all-India tolerance and eclecticism, stressing the peaceful coexistence of different religions, ethnic groups, and life styles and criticizing the parochial and intolerant. The language-specific Mass Culture stresses tolerance and eclecticism between groups within the language area, but it also stresses the superiority of its cultural heritage, *its* heroes, and *its* language.
5. With the decline of the princely states and the abolition of the zamindars, Patronage Culture in India is diminishing for lack of a target audience. The decline of traditional patrons will have little effect on India's overall artistic productivity if national institutes and academic centers provide an alternative environment for artists to develop Artist Culture.
6. Adherents of Artist Culture have mixed feelings toward Mass Culture. A few "missionary" artists hope to uplift Mass Culture, but most artists fear that Mass Culture will debase "true art" and that participating in Mass Culture will de-professionalize one. Ravi Shankar's current anomalous status among Indian musicians is a case in point.
7. Mass Culture borrows and standardizes elements from Artist Culture. In so doing, it introduces large sections of the population to Artist Culture for the first time. In this manner, in the long run, Mass Culture contri-

butes to the support of and recruitment into Artist Culture, even while, in the short run, it appears to "debase" it.

8. Artist Culture will continue to be regarded as of higher status than Mass Culture. Persons wishing to impress others with their good taste will continue to support Artist Culture in preference to Mass Culture.[7]

9. Mass Culture borrows and standardizes elements from Folk/Community Culture. Given the tenuousness of Folk/Community Culture, Mass Culture probably poses a serious threat to it. Just as in the United States the cinema, radio, and television spelled the end of the local talent show; so in India one can predict these same phenomena will spell the end of the bard, the *bhana*, and many of the other folk artists. A few folk artists will make the transition to Mass Culture; the rest will disappear for lack of clientele. And Folk/Community Culture audiences will experience continuing pressures to become part of the Public.

10. Under certain circumstances, especially when their language and identity are threatened, Folk/Community Cultures will actively reject their absorption into Mass Culture. A case in point are the Santal tribals in Bihar. In an effort to keep from blending into the greater Hindu Sanskritic tradition, they activated their Folk/Community Culture, developed their own Santal epic, created their Santal script, and self-consciously set themselves apart as a unique cultural group.[8]

One might predict similar resistance patterns elsewhere in

---

7. I have been told of Bengali weddings in which the type of recorded music played over the loudspeaker reflected the family's status. Thus, highest-status families played only classical *shanai* (a reed instrument) recording throughout the festivities. Slightly lower families played *shanai* records at key moments during the wedding ceremony and Bengali songs the rest of the time. Still lower families added Hindi songs to the Bengali songs. And the lowest families played exclusively Hindi film songs through the celebrations.

8. See Martin Orans, *The Santal: A Tribe in Search of a Great Tradition*, Detroit: Wayne State University Press, 1965.

India, especially on the part of Indian tribal groups, or certain majority-rejecting groups like the neo-Buddhist Mahars.

11. This overarching process of absorbing Folk/Community Cultures into more encompassing types of culture and introducing the more encompassing type of culture back into the Folk/Community Cultures is a continuation of the interplay between various "Little Traditions," "Intermediate Traditions," and "Great Traditions" that has gone on for centuries. The mass media may speed up and intensify the process, but the process has been a part of Indian life for centuries and will probably continue to be so for many years to come.

3

LANGUAGE AND MASS COMMUNICATION IN INDIA

Franklin C. Southworth

In most parts of India today, various forms of language are in competition with each other for the attention of the public. These forms range from the extremely informal, near-colloquial style of speech found in radio "soap operas" and the cinema, to the formal and highly literary styles of the newspapers and news broadcasts. The varieties of language currently in use have distinct histories; they perform different functions in the society, and (as employed by the mass media) they reach partially different audiences. In most of the linguistic regions the "standard" languages are currently undergoing "development" and their ultimate shape is subject to a variety of forces. It is appropriate to ask what these forces are, what effects they can be expected to have on the languages themselves, and how effectively they are employed by the mass media. These are questions which cannot be answered in detail for any of the regional languages at present. Still, it is possible to explore some of the factors involved, and uncover areas requiring further study. The following discussion is divided into three parts: (1) varieties of language and their communicative roles in Indian society; (2) regional languages in mass communication; (3) implications and suggestions for research.

VARIETIES OF LANGUAGE AND THEIR COMMUNICATIVE ROLES IN INDIAN SOCIETY

History

We have no information about the existence of any languages which might have been used for purposes of mass communication in the older period. Trade languages of some sort may have existed, but they have left no traces. Evidence of regional variation in North India from as early as the third century B.C., exists in the Ashokan inscriptions; there is evidence of social variation as well. Since the documents that have survived are mainly of a literary, religious, or official nature, they tell us little or nothing about the language of the masses in that period. Material in the Prakrit languages appears to have been restricted to particular regions, just as were the documents which have been given the names of the modern vernaculars (Old Marathi, Old Tamil, Old Bengali, etc.).

The only language which had any supra-regional pretensions was apparently Sanskrit, used all over India by Brahmans and members of other twice-born castes. Sanskrit, of course, never was a vehicle of mass communication; in fact, those who used the language took care that only the elite gained access to it. Tradition tells us that Sanskrit was taught to the sons (not the daughters) of upper-caste families, in circumstances which prevented even accidental attendance by individuals of lower castes. (This was usually done in the house of the Brahman *guru*, which could not be approached by members of lower castes.) That the language had to be taught in this way implies that from a very early period, Sanskrit was a non-native language for all of those who used it. Just as Vedic was used for ritual purposes, Sanskrit was used for all the formal occasions of life.

Though perhaps the most important social function of Sanskrit education was to propagate an elite language, the society of the time defended the study of Sanskrit for other reasons. Thus Patanjali, a grammarian of the first century B.C., tells us that the study of grammar has as its purpose the preservation of the Veda, the learning of proper language for use in sacrifice, the avoidance of barbaric speech, and the preservation of one's proper status; he tells us, furthermore, that the correct observance of grammatical rules leads to heaven, whereas the use of improper grammar can lead to defeat, ineffectiveness of sacrifice and, in some cases, death.[1]

1. Kshitish Chandra Chatterji, *Patanjali' Mahabhashya: Paspasahnika* (introductory chapter), Calcutta: A. Mukherjee and Co., 1965, p. 5ff.

These attitudes toward the social functions of language have implications for vernacular education and mass media in the modern context, as will be seen later.

Presumably, the political climate of the early period, with its many small political units and constantly shifting allegiances, discouraged the development of supraregional standard languages or lingua francas (except possibly in some commercial contexts), just as the social structure apparently inhibited the development of linguistic varieties which would allow easy communication among different social levels. The first known case of a genuinely supraregional language was Urdu, or (as the nonliterary form used to be called) Hindustani Urdu, the language of the Mogul armies and later of the North Indian bazaars. This language still survives, of course, as a standard literary language and in the form of a middle- and lower-class colloquial lingua franca in the North. When English education was introduced to India, English rapidly became the all-India elite language, replacing Persian and Urdu in the North, and Sanskrit elsewhere. The new English education may to some extent have redefined the limits of the elite group, but there was never any question of English being a mass language at that time.

Linguistic Varieties

The study of linguistic variation[2] involves a fascinating interplay of three theoretically different, but actually overlapping types of variation: regional, social, and functional. Functional

---

2. For descriptions of various types of linguistic variation in South Asia see Mahadeo L. Apte, "Linguistic Acculturation and Its Relation to Urbanization and Socioeconomic Factors," *Indian Linguistics,* 1962, 23:5-25; William Bright (ed.) *Sociolinguistic* (Proceedings of the UCLA Sociolinguistics Conference), The Hague: Mouton and Co., 1964; Charles A. Ferguson, and John J. Gumperz (eds.) *Linguistic Diversity in South Asia: Studies in Regional, Social, and Functional Variation. International Journal of American Linguistics,* 26.3, Part III. Bloomington, 1960; M. Shanmugam Pillai, "Caste Isoglosses in Kinship Terms," *Anthropological Linguistics,* 1965, 7: 59-66; and A. K. Ramanujan, "The Structure of Variation: A Study in Caste Dialects," in Milton Singer and Bernard S. Cohn (eds.) *Structure and Change in Indian Society,* Chicago: Aldine Publishing Company, 1968, pp. 461-74.

variation, which is the type perhaps least noticed by non-linguists, involves the use of different *registers* of a language (sometimes even different languages) by the same individual or group for different social functions. This type of variation is very old in Indian society: the modern-day distinctions found, for example, in Bengali and Tamil between the informal, colloquial register and the quite distinct register of formal oratory, are comparable to the traditional distinction between Sanskrit (either the literary form used for writing, formal debates, etc., or the Vedic ritual language used for talking to the Gods) and Prakrit, used for the casual routine of daily life.

Western societies do not really have any counterpart to this, even though there is considerable difference between the usual spoken and written forms of many western languages. At its most extreme, one might compare the Indian situation to that which would obtain in present-day English-speaking society, if all writing had to be done in the language of Shakespeare or that of the King James version of the Bible. For all but the most educated individuals, this leads to a situation where a person has only partial (and mainly passive) control over the formal register — comparable to the partial understanding of Shakespearean language possessed by most American college students, or to the passive knowledge of the special Biblical vocabulary (e.g., *begat, quoth, verily*) and morphology *(thou art, he gaveth)* prevalent among English-speaking Protestants. This linguistic "double standard", in which most Indians participate to some extent, is of crucial importance in determining the form of standard languages, as will be seen below.

Each of the major linguistic regions of the subcontinent is fragmented into a fantastic array of local and subregional dialects, as can be seen in Grierson's *Linguistic Survey of India*. Within each variety, usage also varies considerably along social lines, with the lowest caste groups being most divergent and isolated linguistically in all parts of the country.[3] In some

---

3. See John J. Gumperz, "Dialect Differences and Social Stratification in a North Indian Village," *American Anthropologist,* 1958, 60:668-82; Apte, 1962 for Maharashtra; and William McCormack, "Social Dialects in Dharwar Kannada," in Ferguson and Gumperz, op. cit.

areas, particularly in Maharashtra and the South, Brahmans also speak a distinctive variety of the regional language.[4] This probably reflects a historical situation in which there was little or no direct communication between the traditional elites and the lowest castes, though intermediate groups communicated with those of higher as well as lower rank.[5] These intermediate groups also differ somewhat from each other,[6] but usually less so than the highest and lowest groups do, so that for the bulk of the population there is a continuum of variations without sharp breaks. Differences also occur between male and female speech, but mainly because the speech of uneducated village women is generally restricted to the immediate local dialect, whereas a man who is at all mobile generally learns to use some supraregional variety in addition to his native speech.

In each linguistic region, there are (at least potentially) three types of language which function as "standards" (using this term in the general sense of supraregional or supraclass variety which is superimposed on local and social varieties). These are: the *regional literary standards*, most of which have been created in the nineteenth and twentieth centuries; the *educated colloquial varieties* used by the politically dominant, more mobile, and increasingly urban-based regional elites; and the *bazaar languages* (or commercial lingua francas), used by a broad spectrum of social groups for trade and related purposes.

Regional literary standards developed mainly during the nineteenth century, in some cases under the direct stimulus of the British, although also from contemporary or earlier vernacular literature. Vernacular literature was in direct competition with English in the educational, literary, and journalistic spheres; writers were under pressure from the beginning to show that their languages were equal, or superior to, English in beauty and expressive power. The models before these writers were the upper-echelon ICS men, military officers, and

---

4. Apte, 1962; Ramanujan, 1968.
5. Franklin C. Southworth, "Detecting Prior Pidginization: An Analysis of the Historical Origin of Marathi," in Dell Hymes (ed.) *Pidginization and Creolization of Languages,* London: Cambridge University Press, 1971, pp. 255-74.
6. Gumperz, 1958; and Pillai, 1965.

company executives, who wrote the flawless English of the public school graduate, and who knew their English classics thoroughly. Under the circumstances, it is not surprising that the Indian literary ideal often appears to prize beauty of expression over clarity, the impeccable turn of phrase over directness, and purity of language (the word chaste constantly recurs in discussions of language in India) over communicative power. The English of the classics was prized by Englishmen as a symbol of their culture; the Indian literati strove to create (or, in their eyes, often to perpetuate) a language which would be equally expressive, equally literary, and (when the occasion demanded) equally complex and obscure. Since the development of regional languages was intially under the control of the traditional elites, the forms which these languages took reflected not only the usage of the elite groups, but also their puristic and exclusive traditions, and their tendency to draw on the great standard of the past, Sanskrit, for their lexical resources. This was true of the Dravidian languages as well as the Indo-Aryan in the early period; the only exception was Urdu, which as a literary language drew on Persian and Arabic models.

A particular specimen of written language can be said to possess a certain *degree of literariness;* that is, some specimens are more literary than others. Personal letters, for example, tend nowadays to use a fairly informal variety of the language, even though their style may still be literary compared to the spoken language. Some writers even speak of "hybrid styles" of written language, which combine a literary with an informal colloquial style.[7] There is, to be honest, a good deal of loose talk on this subject, and there have been no attempts to develop any measures of literariness so that such judgments could be quantified. It would be quite possible to develop such measures, e.g. in terms of grammatical complexity (number of subordinate clauses, length of sentences, etc.), vocabulary selection, or ease of comprehension. Until we are ready to submit our

---

7. M.W.S. De Silva, "Convergence in Diglossia: The Sinhalese Situation," in Franklin C. Southworth and Mahadeo L. Apte (eds.) *Contact and Convergence in South Asian Languages* (forthcoming); See also K. V Subbarao, "Varieties of Telugu," (Unpublished paper), Bloomington.

judgments to measurements of this type, much of our discussions on this subject will be only impressionistic.

Educated colloquial standards exist for most of the major regional languages, but these have so far been inadequately studied. Linguists (both native and foreign) have worked to some extent on the description of these varieties, but have often gone astray because they did not pay enough attention to social and functional variation. In some cases, they have too readily accepted the notion of native speakers that the canons of the literary form apply equally to the spoken form: in other cases they have been content to study a single variety (usually the speech of a highly educated and very articulate group in rather formal situations), without examining varieties used by other groups or in other speech situations. In any case, some educated colloquial standards do exist, though we do not know enough about the elasticity of their rules or how widely they are used. In most areas, the colloquial standard is said to be based on the variety of a particular subregion of greater linguistic prestige: for the Hindi region, the prestige area is eastern Uttar Pradesh (particularly the cities of Lucknow, Allahabad, and Banaras); for Marathi, it is the Bombay-Poona area; for Malayalam, it is the central part of Palghat District (i.e., the old Walluvanad Taluk) in South Malabar. Literary standards also tend to be closely related to the elite speech of these prestige areas, though perhaps not as much as people believe. Careful investigation of the prestige areas might well reveal that the prestige norm is actually realized only in the speech of a small number of highly educated (male) scholars and literati of the older generation — and mainly when these gentlemen are on their best linguistic behavior.

Bazaar languages, or trade languages, develop from the requirements of transactions and thus cross social as well as regional barriers. Institutions such as the armed forces and government offices, which require communication among people of diverse social and regional backgrounds, show a similar linguistic development. Bazaar Hindustani, in current use throughout the urban centers of north India, and to some extent in the South, is this type of language. (The lingua franca of retired military men throughout India is Hindustani, and English in addition for the officers). It is probable that there exist, in all the linguistic regions, trade languages of this sort which have the same function for the uneducated that the elite colloquial language has for the educated; these have not, however, been adequately studied, so that we do not know how widely a particular variety is used, nor how it compares to the educated colloquial language in terms of intelligibility. It is clear, however, that because of the circumstances of their use, trade languages differ from the "higher" forms of language in two ways: (1) they are much less influenced by notions of linguistic "purity" (for example, individuals communicating in these varieties seldom, if ever, criticize each other for mistakes in grammar, whereas this is not uncommon among educated speakers); (2) these varieties may function as *partial languages*, used only for specific purposes, and may not cover the total range of a person's communicative needs. A bazaar language often functions as a second variety for the village man, in his commercial and social dealings outside his own village; the village woman is much less likely to control a second variety.

Current Attitudes and Language "Development"

Along with the persistence of traditional types of linguistic variation, many traditional attitudes toward language have also survived. The purism of the traditional elites, which has served to limit access to the elite group, has been mentioned above. The "double standard" of functional variation also has been mentioned. In the present context, it may be useful to view this type of variation in terms of a conflict between two opposed (but not incompatible) functions of language, the *ritualistic* and *communicative*. In most informal kinds of speech situations, where questions of relative status of participants are of minimal importance, one is most concerned with interaction and the transmission of messages appropriate to that interaction; in such a situation we could say that the communicative function is dominant. At the opposite pole from such situations are those occasions where the primary concern is the uttering of prescribed and propitious words in the most correct and appropriate way; such occasions would include religious ceremonies, formal speeches, and numerous academic activities such as classroom recitation and examinations. Many activities, of course, involve both of these functions, and they are not necessarily always in conflict. There are, however, situations where conflicts do appear to arise.

The situation is further complicated by the fact that Indians, in spite of the linguistic variation going on around them, appear to have the same sort of conceptual model of linguistic behavior that most westerners have: in general, they behave as though there were just *one* Hindi, just *one* Tamil, just *one* English etc. Although the professional linguist might describe the situation as characterized by a multiplicity of linguistic standards, each appropriate to a particular class of situations, the participant in these situations appears to believe that there is a single standard, but that situations differ in the extent to which they constrain him to observe the grammatical niceties of his language. Thus, if a speaker's attention is called to some usage which is in conflict with the grammatical rules of the literary standard, his reaction might be "oh yes, that's the way one *should* say it, but sometimes we don't bother," or else "oh, those fellows don't really speak the language." This normative type of judgment seems somewhat unusual, in view of the ready acceptance of the existence of separate norms in other areas of activity, such as dress or eating.

This attitude towards language can also be easily manipulated, in the same way that religious intolerance can be manipulated, for political ends. Ellen McDonald has pointed out that the development of a regional literary standard in Maharashtra was closely linked with the growth of regional consciousness in that area.[8] Similar activities were going on in other linguistic areas, involving the organization of historical and language societies for the purpose of carrying out research in the regional language and literature.[9] McDonald discusses in

---

8. See Elen E. McDonald, "The Growth of Regional Consciousness in Maharashtra," *Journal of the Indian Economic and Social History Review*, 1968, 5:223-43.

9. Jyotirindra Das Gupta and John J. Gumperz, "Language, Communication and Control in North India," in J. A. Fishman, C. A. Ferguson. and J. Das Gupta (eds.) *Language Problems of Developing Nations,* New York: John Wiley and Sons, 1968, pp. 151-66.

some detail the relationship between such activities and the political ambitions of the regional elites; although the shape of these elite groups has changed to some extent since the nineteenth century, the manipulation of language norms has survived as a political strategy in creating a local power base for the elites.

Similar remarks could be made about the situation in Tamil Nadu, though in this case the development of the regional standard was linked with an anti-Brahman movement and the creation of a new political elite.[10] The now prestigious Sen Tamil, a de-Sanskritized (in comparison with the formerly prestigious Brahman version) language which depends on classical Tamil for its lexical resources, is now the literary standard of Tamil Nadu as well as the state language of education. It is also a highly visible symbol of the new political forces in the region, because of its manifest rejection of the Indo-Aryan North, along with the Sanskrit of the Brahmans. Though this language is politically useful, it poses problems for the Tamilian school child from an illiterate family, who does not find it easy to learn the standard language. (Many fail the SSLC examination in Tamil.) For the person whose knowledge is limited to a nonelite colloquial variety of the language, it appears to make little difference whether he is required to learn a Sanskritized or a classificalized literary form in school.

Since literary standards function to facilitate communication among people whose spoken usage differs appreciably from each other, educated elites often use this function to justify the propagation and "development" of the literary standard as the sole medium of education and public writing. Das Gupta and Gumperz have discussed the way in which this attitude on the part of scholars has led to extreme Sanskritization in the case of the Hindi literary standard, and how this has contributed to making this language much more inaccessible to the ordinary speaker of Hindi.[11] Similar developments have

---

10. Robert L. Hardgrave, Jr., *The Dravidian Movement*, Bombay: Popular Prakashan, 1965, p. 30.

11. Das Gupta and Gumperz, op. cit., p. 163: "It seems evident that the new differences between colloquial and literary Hindi resulting from

been and are still taking place in other parts of the country, for substantially the same reasons, and it seems very unlikely in the present situation that any alternative policy (such as propagating varieties of language which are closer to the colloquial varieties) would be considered — or even adequately investigated. Politically, the Sanskritized Hindi may serve as a symbol of the fall of British (as well as Muslim) sovereignty, but this would appear to be of small comfort to a man who wants his children to be educated so that they can get jobs; significantly, this "nationalistic" argument is most vigorously propounded by politicians and other elites, who in any case are able to send their children to English medium schools.

REGIONAL LANGUAGES IN MASS COMMUNICATION

The aspects of mass communication which will be considered here are as follows: journalism, radio and television, the cinema, mass education, literature and other public writing, and the use of language (both spoken and written) for purposes of political propaganda. These do not perhaps exhaust the uses of language in mass communication, but will provide a sufficient variety of contexts in which the role of the various languages may be examined.

Journalism

From their beginnings, English and vernacular newspapers in India were aimed at (partially) different audiences, but in both cases, access to them has been limited to small literate groups. Readership has increased enormously in recent years with the growing rate of literacy, but on the whole, there does not seem to have been any substantial attempt to increase circulation by simplifying the written style of most papers, e.g. by using more familiar vocabulary or shorter sentences. (This is a general impression gained by examining newspapers in

---

recent language reform materially add to the ordinary speaker's task of learning literary Hindi ... these who have been exposed to the present form of literary Hindi as part of their family background have considerable advantage in the educational system.''

Hindi, Marathi, Tamil, and Malayalam, and from interviews with journalists and readers from these and other language areas.) If anything, it seems likely that there has been a general trend since independence toward making the style *more literary* and therefore *less accessible* to the person with minimal literacy, at least in the longer-established papers. A few of the newer papers, especially those with a non-Congress orientation (such as the DMK *Dinattandi* in Tamil, and the Communist *Deshabhimani* in Malayalam), appear to be trying to give their language a slightly more popular flavor, but even in these cases the language is quite close to the literary standard in terms of vocabulary and grammatical complexity. This appears to be true even in the case of papers which are not aimed at the sophisticated, educated populations of urban areas; e.g. the weekly *Adivasi*, which is aimed at tribal and low-caste groups in the Ranchi area, uses a Hindi as Sanskritized as that of any of the urban dailies. In several areas, there is a noticeable trend to publish local news in a less literary style than national or international news. In fact, I gained the impression from conversations with taxi drivers and shopkeepers in Delhi, that only the local news is read in detail, whereas for their knowledge of the larger events, they appeared to depend on a few cue words in the headlines, supplemented by conversations with acquaintances. The same may well be true of other less-educated readers.

Reports from rural parts of the Hindi area indicate that there is, on the whole, very little reading of newspapers. Except for those areas within close proximity of the big cities, it appears to be uncommon to find more than a handful of people in a village who see a newspaper with any regularity. News is generally spread by word of mouth, though the radio is now becoming an increasingly important source. By all accounts this is the situation in most of rural India, with the exception of Kerala; there, partly because of a higher rate of literacy (and perhaps because of other factors), it is not uncommon to find daily newspaper readings, attended by a high percentage of the village men (especially the younger ones). The high level of interest in political developments may of course relate to the greater degree of political awareness of the population, especially the poorer and less educated segment. In the absence of research data, it is impossible to say how much news is understood by the average listener, but comprehension is at any rate sufficient to maintain a fairly high level of interest. This is true in spite of the fact that literary Malayalam is highly Sanskritized, and quite distinct from colloquial varieties.[12]

The Kerala example suggests that the degree of literariness of newspaper language is not the only factor which determines comprehensibility; motivational factors must also be taken into account, and these appear to include the desire to know (as determined by economic and other needs), and perhaps also the social value of news as a topic of conversation.

The linguistic behavior of journalists can be explained better in terms of their attitudes toward language than toward readers or potential readers. The behavior of any editors appears to be guided by the old need to uphold literary standards for vernacular literature, which in the early days of journalism had to compete with English. One reason for suspecting this is the variation in style between local and other news items, mentioned above. All international news, and much of the national news, reaches the newspaper offices in English and must be translated, whereas the local news is often gathered by a reporter in the regional language. The process of translating from English has some of the properties of a literary exercise, and the presence of the English model may encourage a search for linguistic resources which the editor considers equivalent to theh English. The obvious source for such literary devices is the regional literary language, and there now exist dictionaries (English-Hindi, English-Tamil, etc.) which appear to have been designed for just this purpose, since they were created by inventing Sanskrit (or other) equivalents for

---

12. Joan P. Mencher, "Politics, Religion and Caste in Madras Villages: An Analysis of Their Interrelations and Implications for Development." Paper presented at the 67th annual meeting of the American Anthropological Association, November 1968, now being revised for publication. This information on rural Kerala is from Joan P. Mencher and P. Kunhikannan (of Cannanore District, Kerala).

English technical and literary terms for use in the regional languages.

A member of the editorial staff of a Hindi daily in Delhi informed me that his superiors, and many of his colleagues, appear to believe that they have a role to play in uplifting their language and maintaining a proper standard of literary respectability, and that this takes precedence over making the language more accessible to the public. I have heard similar attitudes expressed by Marathi journalists. These few chance conversations do not substitute, of course, for a systematic survey of attitudes. One further point of evidence should be recorded, however: in my own reading (and this is corroborated by other students of Indian languages), I have found the language of editorials generally to be the most difficult, with respect to grammatical complexity and vocabulary selection. This appears to correlate with another observation, that editorials are the least read (or in any case, the least discussed) parts of most Indian vernacular papers. All of this evidence, for what it is worth, appears to strengthen the argument that the editors of newspapers, as a group, tend to identify themselves with those scholars who have taken it upon themselves to "develop" their languages by removing them as far as possible from the vulgar usage of the masses.

Radio

Radio and television have great potential in mass communication, because their coverage is not limited to the literate population. On the other hand, both are under government control, which means that they are instruments of official language policy. The range of programs currently being broadcast over the radio includes a wide variety of informational and educational programs, as well as cultural and entertainment programs aimed at a broad spectrum of tastes. An important question to be asked is whether the type of language used is appropriate to the material being broadcast, and to the audience for which it is intended; a superficial examination of a few areas would suggest that it is not always as appropriate as it might be.

In the summer of 1969, an informal sampling of Hindi programs was done in Delhi.[13] The sample showed a range of linguistic styles from near-colloquial (e.g. in some of the dramas on the program *havaa mahal*) to highly formal, literary style (e.g. news broadcasting and lectures on cultural topics). Several educated informants described the latter variety as "difficult," and one person (an M.A. in Hindi) said that although he could understand everything, it required quite a lot of concentration to understand all the details — even in a news broadcast. Information programs (such as those dealing with agricultural development or family planning) aimed at popular audiences were in a less formal style, sometimes approaching the colloquial, but still quite different from ordinary conversation. Broadcasts on the *krisi jagat* (agricultural) program, for example, were supposed to consist of long artificial monologues which lacked the flow of normal conversation.

For the rural part of the Hindi area, a village in Madhya Pradesh studied by Doranne Jacobson in the mid-1960's, may be a useful specimen to look at. There were three radios in the village, all owned by Muslims. Jacobson herself had a radio, and the only person in the village who ever asked to listen to the news broadcast in Hindi was the Brahman postmaster, a man with a traditional Sanskrit education. She considered it unlikely that anyone in the village, other than the few educated Brahmans, could understand the radio news. (Apart from the local dialect, known by all the villagers, most of the village men could communicate in the bazaar variety.) Most news in the village travelled by word of mouth; the original source might be a passing truck driver who stopped at the village tea shop, or a village man returning from Bhopal (forty miles distant) who had picked up some news from a hotel there.[14] The fact that the original source of the news, in either of these cases, was often a radio, indicates that the radio has at least a great potential use.

13. This sampling was undertaken in connection with the preparation of a *Student's Hindi-Urdu Reference Manual,* under a grant from the U.S. Office of Education.

14. Dr. Doranne Jacobson, City University of New York (personal communication).

A sampling of Tamil radio programs in Madras in 1966-67 shows a similar range of usage, from very formal to very colloquial. Dramas were often in a highly colloquial style, usually the elite colloquial, but one program (*kaappukatti cattram*) intended to depict village life, made use of imitations of other social and regional variants. The language of some of the agricultural programs was also quite informal, and often in a good facsimile of conversational style; this was understood by illiterate farmers in a village in which I worked, and in fact at least one of them began to use new agricultural inputs as a result of information obtained from this program. Though the news broadcasts were in a highly formal style, the local school-masters and several other older educated men listened to them regularly. (It may be relevant to note that several of these men were very active politically, mainly in the DMK party.) During this period, many villages in the area had Panchayat radios, often equipped with loudspeakers for public listening. Their main output was film music, and many of the younger village people (especially females) not only listened avidly to these and learned them, but were also familiar with the names of the films and the singers, and occasionally paid some attention to the commentaries interspersed between the songs by the radio announcer. This aspect of mass culture has been observed in all parts of India, but I know of no attempts to measure its effectiveness (or its potential impact) as a medium of communication.

There would appear to be a clear need to study the comprehensibility of radio language, in terms of the audiences for which particular programs are intended. It is significant that this has not yet been undertaken to any extent. Another useful point for study would be the extent of correlation between the style of particular broadcasts, and the social and educational backgrounds of the individuals (announcers, writers, program and station directors) responsible for those broadcasts.

Television

Television and the cinema, in addition to being nonliterary media, have the additional advantage of being able to use visual cues to reinforce the information being presented in spoken form. These additional cues can often compensate for dialectal differences between speakers and hearers. Television is currently in operation only in the area of greater Delhi and other major cities but plans are now being made for an experimental communications satellite to be used for broadcasting to several "backward" areas. The potential of television as an educational device is very great, but exploiting this potential depends among other things on resolving some of the above mentioned problems about the choice of appropriate language.

The Cinema

The language of the cinema appears to be, on the whole, more accessible to the average man than that of other media. The Hindi movies, for example, make considerable use of the colloquial style of speech formerly known as Hindustani — which contains many more words of Perso-Arabic origin than the official Hindi, and is closer to the normal colloquial language of western U.P. than to the so-called *suddh,* "pure", Hindi literary language based on the elite speech of eastern U.P. On the other hand, the presence of nonverbal cues makes it difficult to assess the importance of the role of language in the cinema. It appears possible to understand much of a Hindi movie even without knowing much Hindi, and the popularity of Hindi movies (along with the movie songs) in many areas attests to this. Thus, mere attendance is not a guarantee of linguistic comprehension. Short of interviewing people in detail it is difficult to imagine what criteria could be used for testing comprehension; for example, the amount of laughter provoked by a joke cannot be a criterion unless one can eliminate other cues (gestures, facial expressions, etc.) as possible reasons for the laughter. The language of the cinema, like that of other media, also shows considerable variation along the informal-formal dimension. In Tamil movies, the language varies from near colloquial (e.g., in social dramas and comic passages) to rather formal (e.g., in pictures on historical-mythological themes). Some variation in Hindi films is also reported by informants, but no systematic study of such variation has been undertaken to my knowledge. It seems possible that, for many cinema-goers, a state of partial comprehension is accepted and inevitable, at least part of the time; the situation here can perhaps be likened to certain ritualistic types of activities in the society, which involve passive participation. Thus, for example, the speech of a mythological hero may often be less important than the visual background against which it takes place.

To the extent that cinema language is closer to informal popular speech, two factors would seem to be of the greatest importance: (1) the need to appeal to mass audiences, i.e. basically a commercial motivation; (2) the portrayal of everyday situations, in which the popular language is more appropriate than the more formal variety. It is important to bear in mind also that, in the village context, the cinema competes with other forms of entertainment which use a more popular language, sometimes even the local dialect, in order to obtain the most direct contact with the audiences. A case in point is Mencher's discussion of a festival (*kuttu*) held in a Tamil village in 1957.[15] This festival was of religious significance, and had political implications for the dominant Nayakar caste of the village; it involved, in addition to religious processions, a dramatic portrayal of some scenes from the *Mahabharata*. Apart from being a source of popular entertainment, the festival was important for the caste leaders in that it reaffirmed the Nayakars' claim of descent from the Pandavas (the heroes of the *Mahabharata*). During the course of the festival, it was observed that the dramatic scenes, which involved a use of popular (sometimes rather racy) language, were well-attended, whereas the reciting of passages in classical Tamil were attended mainly by village elders. Most of the villagers who were questioned about this maintained that the recitations were an important part of the festival, and that they enjoyed and understood them; but somehow, they found it necessary to do other work during those times.

Education

Formal public education is one of the most powerful tools

---

15. See Mencher, 1968.

for influencing linguistic norms, as well as linguistic attitudes. The above discussion about language "development" gives an indication of the role being played by education in this regard. In general, the official medium of instruction, and the language of textbooks and examinations, is the regional literary standard. It is true, of course, that in many areas the regional language gives way to the local dialect as the medium of instruction, at least in the elementary grades (though teachers are normally reluctant to admit this). Nevertheless, it is impossible to obtain instruction in any subject without first acquiring a command of the literary language, since this is the language of textbooks and examinations; this factor is currently a significant bottleneck in the educational process, which prevents all but a small minority from getting through school. Currently, there seem to be only a few attempts underway to use any other approach to the language of education; these are mostly in special programs, such as those for adult literacy. An example of this is Literacy House in Lucknow, a private organization founded by Mrs. Welthy Fisher; many of its publications make use of an informal, nonliterary style without excessive Sanskritization or a high degree of grammatical complexity. Since programs of this type are intended for special circumstances, it is unlikely that even a high degree of success would have any effect on general language policy for public education. In fact, it seems likely that public policy in this regard is influenced primarily by political factors of the type discussed above, and is hardly affected at all by any sort of negative feedback from the participants (students, parents, and teachers).

Literature

The language of contemporary literature is highly variable as regards the formal-informal dimension: although traditionally the formal style is always used in literary material, nowadays it is not at all uncommon to see an informal colloquial style used in fiction. The informal style is used extensively in dialogues, and has been for some time, but it can also be found in descriptive passages as well.[16] It would be of interest to examine the correlations of style and subject matter in contemporary literature, but I do not know of this having been done in any systematic way for any language. Apart from this, the impact of literature in the context of mass communication is very difficult to assess, without figures on circulation of various periodicals or sale of books. If such figures could be obtained for rural as well as urban areas, their changes over time might give valuable indications of trends in the use of language, as well as the impact of education on literacy.

Public Writing

The written language of public signs, notices, and advertisements, as well as that of official decrees and government propaganda, appears to follow in general the norms of formal-literary style; in fact, some of the most extreme forms of pedantic language are found in such documents. Das Gupta and Gumperz have mentioned the extremely Sanskritized style of public documents in Hindi,[17] and parallels can be found in many of the other regional languages. In Madras, for example, I observed signs in classical Tamil in government offices in 1969, containing information which had been given in English previously (e.g., during my previous visit in 1967). The significance of this can be appreciated in the light of another observation made at the same time: the English words on roadsigns indicating mileages on the main road between Madras and Bangalore had been removed for a distance of about twenty miles out of Madras. Public signs of this type are of course highly visible symbols in the political conflict on the national language question, and for this reason one can expect that the style of language used would be that regarded as the "purest" and most respectable.

For all kinds of public writing, the presence of English models (see above) is also a potential factor. Since the establishment of Hindi as the official state language in U.P., for example,

---

16. Some examples of this in contemporary Marathi fiction are discussed in detail in Mahadeo L. Apte, "Contemporary Marathi Fiction: Obscenity or Realism?," *The Journal of Asian Studies,* 1969, 29:55-66.

17. Das Gupta and Gumperz, op. cit., pp. 161-2.

much of the official correspondence in Hindi must be translated by pandits from the original English of the bureaucrats, who have not been trained to write acceptable literary Hindi. Similarly, many advertisements of products in newspapers and on billboards are apparently derived from English originals, then translated into the regional language. The Indian Consulate in New York now uses a letterhead with all information given first in literary Hindi, then in English, but it seems likely that the English was the model for the Hindi. Another example of the same type can be seen currently on the license plates of automobiles in the Delhi area. The place numbers are originally issued with Roman letters and international numerals; when the owners of the cars, either because of their own linguistic chauvinism or out of fear of depredations at the hand of Hindi "patriots", translate these into Hindi, the letter sequences are simply converted according to their pronunciation; thus the sequence DLR becomes *Dii el aar*, MPC becomes *em pii sii*, etc. The point of mentioning such observations here is to illustrate the extent to which "translations" of this type are accepted.

In many cases, this type of behavior leads to nothing more than minor inconveniences, though on occasion such a minor matter may be blown up into a major issue because of its political connotations. On the other hand, there are also situations where there is a real conflict between the type of language used and the intended purpose of a document (assuming that the creator of the document actually has some desire to communicate with the intended recipient). Literature on development programs, for example, tends to originate in central or state government bureaucracies, and is often composed originally in English — frequently in a semitechnical or jargonized English, at that. When this is then translated into the regional languages, by translators whose main concern is with the form of the language rather than the linguistic competence of the intended audience (in fact, often without an adequate knowledge of the audience's linguistic usage), it is not surprising that the literature fails to have its intended impact. As an example of this, literature on family planning, which is currently being prepared and distributed in all the regional languages, consists of materials in highly literary language. When I asked some of the workers connected with this program whether villagers could understand the literature that was being distributed, I found that the workers had some difficulty in appreciating the point of my question. The usual reaction was something like: "Of course, we are distributing in all the languages, so that everyone can understand." Apparently no attempt had been made to test the adequacy of the language used before preparing these materials.

The above discussion deals with a number of different factors influencing the degree of formality or "purity" of the regional languages in varying communication situations. These factors may combine in response to the need for greater or lesser "purity." The ideal of linguistic "purity" generally has a stronger influence on written than on spoken language. The type of audience often determines linguistic style. For example, the language of many modern stage plays (intended for sophisticated urban audiences) is generally less popular than that of the cinema or the traditional village entertainment. On the other hand, the medium, rather than the message itself, may be the determining factor. This is the case with newspaper advertisements and the blurbs on product containers (such as soap flakes or breakfast cereals), which are intended for the literate population, and therefore use a highly literary language. Constraints may be imposed by the type of material being transmitted (as in the case of the classicalized language of the Tamil mythological films), or by the source of the message (e.g., the material for news broadcasts, which comes from English sources).

In general, communication appears to be most effective in those cases where there is a mutually beneficial relationship between the sender of a message and the intended audience. There appear to be many situations where the sender of a message does not necessarily see his task primarily in terms of communicating with any audience. As noted above, the use of language in education, in the press, in other public writing, and to some extent on the radio offers many instances of this, though more systematic study would be necessary to obtain reliable estimates of the extent of noncommunication.

In order to devise accurate measures of the communicative potential of different linguistic styles, it would first be necessary to obtain informant judgments of (a) understandability, and (b) acceptability, of a wide variety of materials. Presumably the most useable style for maximal communication would be one which is maximally understandable at various levels of education, without offending too large a percentage of readers because of its lack of "purity." As pointed out above, such judgments can be expected to vary with the nature of the material, and the medium used for transmission. A serious problem in designing such a study is the choice of methods for testing comprehension; since direct formal testing would be unacceptable to most people in the society, it would probably be necessary to use a more lengthy and indirect interview procedure.

In the light of what has been said, what types of change might be anticipated? What predictions can be made about the possible outcome of the conflict of forces described above? On balance, it appears that the forces tending toward greater use of formal language are stronger and more firmly established than those tending in the other direction. Not only are we dealing with a highly stratified society, with all that this implies for restrictions on intergroup communication, but even in cases where an individual's or group's status rises in the social scale, the new status can only be validated by the use of those behavior styles traditionally associated with the elite. This is also true of the newly educated: an educated man must act, dress, and talk like an educated man if he is to be accepted as such. Furthermore, formal education, in the current scheme of things, is increasing the numbers of people who are able to produce and consume material in formal language. In short, as long as a classicalized linguistic norm continues to obtain the support of authority in education and in the mass media, this norm will continue to be the symbol of success. It is conceivable that an increasingly leftist political orientation could lead to some breakdown of the formal-informal dichotomy, but it is hard to believe that this would be anything more than symbolic.

The potential for change, on the other hand, appears to be

slightly greater in some areas than in others. The forces at work on written language appear to be well established and fairly stable, and thus this aspect of language is the least likely to change; the same would appear to be true, in fact, of the cinema, which is at the other end of the linguistic spectrum. The situation in education is also rather stable, though an increased use of films, radio, and television here could possibly lead to some change. The radio, it would seem, is the most free to change, for two reasons: (1) radio language is less rigidly controlled by traditional values, and already displays a considerable amount of variation; (2) policy decisions relating to the radio are quite centralized, as compared with any of the other mass media. Even a change in the relative proportion of programs in informal style might be enough to increase the understandability of many programs, without offending too many people's sensibilities. A greater use of interviews with individuals speaking in more popular styles, could have the effect of giving official sanction to this type of language in certain domains; it would also foster the notion of greater participation of nonelites in public life.

This question need not be thought of in terms of obliterating the formal-informal distinction, since this distinction is thoroughly imbedded in the culture; furthermore, the society offers alternative outcomes: Bengali, for instance, has two "standard" languages, one of which (the *Sadhu bhasa*) is the traditional literary language, and the other (the *colit bhasa*) has been derived in more recent times from a form of elite colloquial.[18] In any case, it is clear that such a change could not take place without an explicit commitment on the part of state governments to reverse the current trend toward greater classicalization.

---

18. Punya Sloka Ray, M. A. Hai, and L. Ray, *Bengali Language Handbook*, Washington: Center for Applied Linguistics, 1966.

4

FORMS AND FUNCTIONS OF MASS MEDIA — THE PRESS

KUSUM NAIR

The focus of this paper is on the effectiveness of newspapers as channels of communication and as instruments of change in the process of modernization in India — more explicitly, on their role in cultural control and in reflecting important changes in mass culture. In all these respects, the role and influence of the press is insignificant and mainly negative. I will cite three examples from my own experience in the field. The first is taken from *Blossoms in the Dust*.[1]

In the first fortnight of January 1959, at Nagpur, the Indian National Congress held its annual session, in itself an important event every year. At this particular session, moreover, the conference adopted certain weighty policy resolutions on agrarian reforms to serve as directives to the governments in the States and at the Centre. In view of the hitherto unsatisfactory progress in the field of agricultural production, it recommended speedy implementation of tenancy reforms, early enactment of ceiling legislation, and adoption of joint farming as the future pattern of farm organisation. It also advised the immediate establishment of rural service co-operatives of various kinds in all villages.

These decisions should have been of intimate concern to

---

1. Kusum Nair, *Blossoms in the Dust,* New York: Frederick A. Praeger, 1961, pp. 124-125. [Footnotes from the quotation have been given serially below for convenience although they appear differently in the original text. Editor.]

every farmer in India, for when implemented they would alter radically not only his economic prospects but also the pattern of his work for generations to come. The pronouncements made headlines in the entire Indian press, and though they provoked a good deal of controversy the Nagpur Conference was acclaimed as historic. But though it is February now, a month after the Nagpur Session, none of the peasants I meet in Rajasthan, barring a few educated middle-class Sikh cultivators in Shri Ganganagar, appear to have heard of the resolutions yet or even that the ruling party has held a conference.[2]

In Daba[3] for instance, a highly prosperous village of 160 families, even though its young *panch* is a member of the local Mandal Committee of the Congress, neither he nor any one else in the village has heard of the Five Year Plan.

It is the same in Kalwad, although this village is only 16 miles distant from the State capital at Jaipur. Set against a background of a ring of low hills littered with stones and small thorny shrubs, Kalwad is a big village and a highly "developed" one; it has 250 irrigation wells, a school building, a tanning and weaving centre, an *ambar charkha* training centre and a credit co-operative society. The latter co-exists with a formidable looking money-lender with heavy gold earrings, to whom most of the villagers are duly indebted. The village is building a *panchayat ghar* and within a year will have a primary health centre. It also has a school with five teachers and 150 pupils, a library, and two wireless sets one of which belongs to the *panchayat*. Even so, none of them has heard of the Congress session at Nagpur. No one

---

2. This despite the fact that under a directive of the Congress, party members had just completed *pad yatras* (walking tours) throughout the country, to contact the rural masses and inform them about the decisions taken at Nagpur Conference.

3. In Nokha Block, Bikaner Division, a village consisting mainly of *Rajputs, Jats, Kumhars* and *Harijans*. Every family has land, including the *Harijans*. The average holding is 100 *bighas*. Like most peasants in these semi-arid areas, they also trade in wool and livestock and actually are better off economically than most of their counterparts in the "wet" regions of Rajasthan.

reads a newspaper[4] and apparently neither of the radios is working.

In Bhoola, a Bhil village in Sirohi district, the villagers admit: "Yes, we have heard of the Congress; yes. Everyone talks of it."

"But," pauses Kania, gravely puckering his bushy eyebrows, "but now that you mention it, we do not know whether Congress is a man or a woman."

Again, Jawaharlal Nehru died on May 27, 1964. In November of that year I was in a village in the district of Salem in Madras State. Yes, they had all heard of 'Nehruji's' death. They had fasted in sorrow. Some had wept. They were still very sad. Six months had elapsed.

"Do you know who the new Prime Minister is?" I asked.

They looked at each other. No. They did not know. Yes, someone had replaced Nehru.

But who?

They did not know his name.

In the third instance, it was in a village in Tanjore district in early 1965. I was talking with a landless agricultural labourer and his wife. They were young. Had three children — one at the breast. The eldest less than three years.

"Do you want any more children?"

"No." They don't. Both are positive.

---

4. Except for one paralytic patient who is a matriculate; but it seems no one else benefits from it. It is not only in the sandy tracts of Rajasthan, however, that there is still such meagre communication of ideas and information. Barring small pockets like Kerala, absence of communication is a conspicuous feature of most of the rural landscape everywhere in India, despite the tremendous improvement of late in the means and modes of transport. As already noted, in the Punjab there is greater mobility and alertness among the peasants than elsewhere and far fewer preservatives of antiquities, such as sand or tradition. But even in the Punjab none of the peasants I met during my tour had heard of the Congress session at Nagpur and of its momentous resolutions, though it was just after the conference had ended. They had not heard of it even in villages with high schools, community radio sets, government Information Centres, and several literates; villages such as Nanheri, Shamspur, Mallehwal and Fatehpur, to name just a few. Apparently, the villagers neither read newspapers nor listen to the news, even if the radio is in working order, as it normally is only if it is privately owned.

"What will you do if another one comes along?"
"I could kill it," the wife replies with some vehemence.
"I could kill it," she repeats. The husband nods.
"Do you know that you can prevent it?"
"Yes. We have heard about it."
"Well. Have you done or are you going to do something about it?"
"No."
"Why not?"
"Oh," replies the husband, "we have heard that if you do, you are liable to die."

An intensive family planning campaign was underway in the district and the state at the time.

II

The masses in India do not read newspapers either because they are illiterate, or because among the few who can read, the majority cannot afford to purchase them. As of the census of 1961 only 24 per cent of the population was literate. Although figures of the 1971 census indicate that the proportion increased over the following decade, it has not increased significantly, and most of the new literates are children still in school. At the least, 70 per cent of the adults are functionally illiterate. In the rural areas, the proportion would be very much higher.

An important clue to the negligible influence of newspapers on the masses lies in the fact that English dailies together still have a larger circulation than dailies in any vernacular including Hindi.

Location of the news media is another indication of the clientele it serves. India has only 107 towns with a population exceeding 100,000, as against 2,583 smaller towns, and some 565,000 villages. With rare exceptions, newspapers are published in only the largest towns.[5] Even so, not all the urban literates read a newspaper.

Uttar Pradesh, for example, has the highest population of

---

5. See Appendix A.

any state of the Indian Union, and also the largest number of towns. Out of a total of 267 towns, only 17 have a population of 100,000 or more. Not a single newspaper is published in a town of less than 100,000 people. As for coverage, whereas 41 per cent of the *urban* population is literate, only 7.18 per cent of them subscribe to a daily; weeklies reach 3.63 per cent.

In West Bengal, urban literacy is 52.9 per cent. Yet, dailies reach only 17.06 per cent of the urban literates, and weeklies, 7.38 per cent. Only three newspapers are located in towns with populations in the range of 50,000 and 100,000.

Even Kerala, with the highest literacy rate, has only three newspapers published in towns of less than 100,000 people. However, 48.79 per cent of the urban literates are covered by newspapers, while weeklies reach 33.07 per cent.

Madras has a vigorous press in English and in Tamil. Not a single paper, however, is published from a town of less than 100,000 population and the dailies cover only 19.03 per cent of the urban literates. Weeklies reach 18.83 per cent.

Similarly, Punjab does not publish any paper in a town of less than 100,000. The dailies cover only 7.48 percent of urban literates, although they constitute 47.7 per cent of the total urban population. Weeklies reach only 1.02 per cent.

These are some of the more developed and progressive states. In Rajasthan, by contrast, urban literacy is 37.6 per cent of the urban population while daily newspapers cover only 1.24 per cent of that population. No newspaper is located in a town of less than 100,000 people.

Comparable figures for the rural areas are not available. But according to a UNESCO survey of comparative levels of mass exposure among peasants in India, out of a sample of 702 persons, only eight had had any exposure to a newspaper or magazine. According to a larger national sample, 22 out of a sample of 7,224 persons had been exposed to a newspaper in 1966.

More important than their geographical location, perhaps, is the fact that most newspapers are managed and edited by men who are virtual strangers to the mass culture. They belong to the urban elite and they cater essentially to the same class of readers. There is a massive gulf between them and the common man, culturally, socially, psychologically. The substance and content of the newspaper, accordingly, has a strong elitist bias. Furthermore, even the vernacular papers generally use the "Presidential" language that is so pure and high-flown that an ordinary literate cannot comprehend it.

Thus, by virtue of its content, language, and location, the press in India cannot be expected to bridge the gulf between the masses and the elite, not even to serve as a mere channel of communication between the literate segments of the two societies. Not only does it not convey urban enlightenment to the illiterate rural masses, but it does not bring news of the latter to the sophisticated urban readers either. Press coverage of the rural areas is extremely poor if not non-existent. The *mofussil* correspondent is generally a resident in the *tehsil* or district headquarters. Typically, he is the local lawyer, and reports mainly about visits of government ministers and other VIPs, the functions held in their honor, and verbatim copies of speeches that embellish such occasions. He is also likely to file official communiques about catastrophies, such as earthquakes and riots.

There is no regular network of professional newspaper correspondents in the countryside to report about economic and political trends and developments, their impact on people and communities, and their responses. When the "Green Revolution" was making headlines in the international press, it was being covered by the national papers in the Indian capital mainly from Parliament Street, from the office of the Press Information Bureau. Consequently, if the rural masses are ignorant of distant happening in the cities, the urban population is equally ignorant about developments in the rural sector.

III

As for serving larger national purpose and goals, the press in India has no power or official sanction as agent of cultural change or modernization — not within even the narrow limits of its clientele. The press in India is a free press, under no government control. There is no *Pravda;* there is nothing akin to the *Dawn* in Karachi.

In the absence of power for the Indian press to influence or induce change, it must be clear on goals, the means of achieving them, and above all, the *desirability* of change. The Indian press is not clear on any of these. It has broad goals. It stands for national independence and international peace. It pontificates with Jesuitical zeal. But there is no commitment, consensus, or identity of outlook between the press and government; within the press, among newspapers; or within a paper itself on specific issues of cultural, attitudinal, or behavioral change. Each newspaper is autonomous and responds differently to whatever the problem or issue.

Basically, the press in India sees itself participating in the democratic process as an organ of political dissent. This was the role that nationalist papers played vis-a-vis the British prior to independence. National newspapers are heavily concentrated in Delhi, not because the masses live there, but because of their interest in the federal government, its ministers, members of parliament, and the bureaucracy. They seek to influence government policies rather than the views or outlook of their readers. Over the past couple of decades, therefore, most newspapers that used to be published in other states (Bombay, Madras, Bengal, etc.) have opened offices in the capital and publish a special Delhi edition.

The most important concern of the press since 1947, in fact, has been defense of editorial freedom — freedom from government; freedom from management; freedom from industrial and commercial interests; freedom from political influence (except for party papers).

According to M. Chalapathi Rau, one of the senior newspaper editors:

> Freedom means responsibility. There can be no true sense of responsibility unless it is responsibility to the public above responsibility to a particular party, to a particular

government, to a particular newspaper, or even to the profession of journalism.[6]

Responsibility to the public, however, is not defined. It can and does, therefore, mean different things to different editors. Furthermore, this freedom, according to Mr. Rau, must extend to the entire staff of a newspaper, and not only to the editor. "Editorial freedom means the freedom of the leader-writer, the freedom of the correspondent, the freedom of the reporter, even the freedom of the sub-editor..."[7]

The test of a good editor and editorial policy accordingly, is conceived as being vigorously independent, objective, impartial, unbiased, uncommitted. However, a conglomeration of such free and disinterested men and editorial policies cannot serve as instruments for forging unity of national purpose or of social and cultural change in a democracy. If, and to whatever extent they do so, it is wholly fortuitous rather than the result of conscious editorial direction.

With regard to interpreting national policies and issues, in effect, Indian newspapers are monuments of confusion, vague rhetoric, and often, total irrelevance. Even if the more progressive ones can claim to create a general climate for modernization, it is so general as to be pointless. However ostensibly virtuous a principle may be, individual behavior is concerned with specifics. And on specifics, a clear message rarely comes through to the average newspaper reader. Even concerning the introduction of a simple innovation like television, the stand of the media can be of astonishing and contrived ambiguity. The *Times of India* of November 2, 1969, for example, carried the following editorial comment on the subject under the caption: "TV or Not TV."

What little Thailand and littler Iraq have, we, the world's largest democracy, must necessarily have, of course. And so, thanks largely to a not entirely disinterested gift from West Germany of hardware and technical assistance, Bombay Poona will have television in some 18 months' time. It

---

6. M. Chalapathi Rau, *Emerging Estate,* New Delhi: Orient Longmans Ltd., 1966, p. 75.
7. Ibid., p. 77.

would be childish to question the propaganda value of this mass communication medium (although the entertainment value is in doubt). Where illiteracy is, as they say, rife, the audio-visual channel can be most effective. But where are the TV sets? Where are the shops and the salesmen to mount high-pressure campaigns so that the customer may get good value for his money by selecting one out of a number of different models? What about after-sales service and the availability of spare parts? Where are the trained and competent repairmen? TV maintenance is far more complicated than the servicing of radio receiving sets (and far costlier). A dead radio set may be ignored as presentable furniture, but a dead TV set will stare at all and sundry, constantly humiliating the owner. Above all, where are our TV artistes? How many have been specially groomed to look well in addition to sounding well? It is clear that hastening to catch up with some other Asian nations we have neglected some of these all-important questions; and hence the question whether to go in for TV in a big way or to plan a little more before embarking on this adventure; as matters stand, we are putting the cart before the bullock.

Obviously, a reader who had never seen television before would find it difficult to decide whether it is good or bad; whether it might be used as a devilish device for official propaganda; whether the artistes would look good or otherwise; and finally, whether he should purchase a set. Whichever way he decided, it would not be on the basis of the *Times of India* editorial.

Similarly, to Kania who is unable to figure out whether Congress is a man or woman, the news media would be of little or no direct assistance even if he were literate. Newspapers are not interested in informing Kania about the Congress. They are preoccupied with telling Congress what it ought or ought not to be.

APPENDIX A

MEDIA PLANNING

Uttar Pradesh

● *Press Media Centres*
★ *Population over 50,000*
■ *Population over 1,00,000*

Mass Culture, Language and Arts in India

Appendix A 65

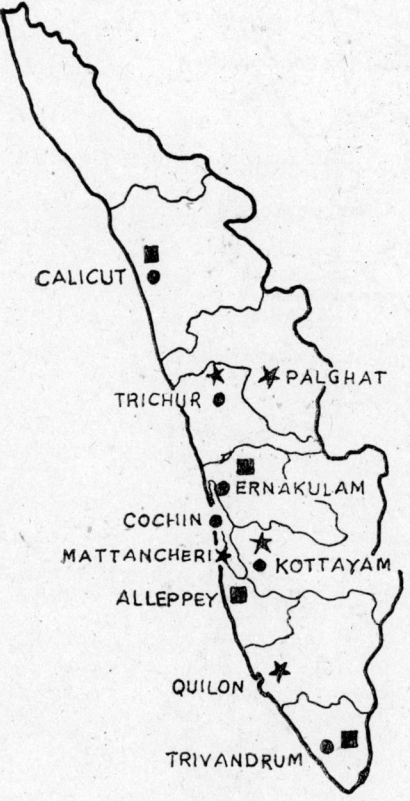

Appendix A

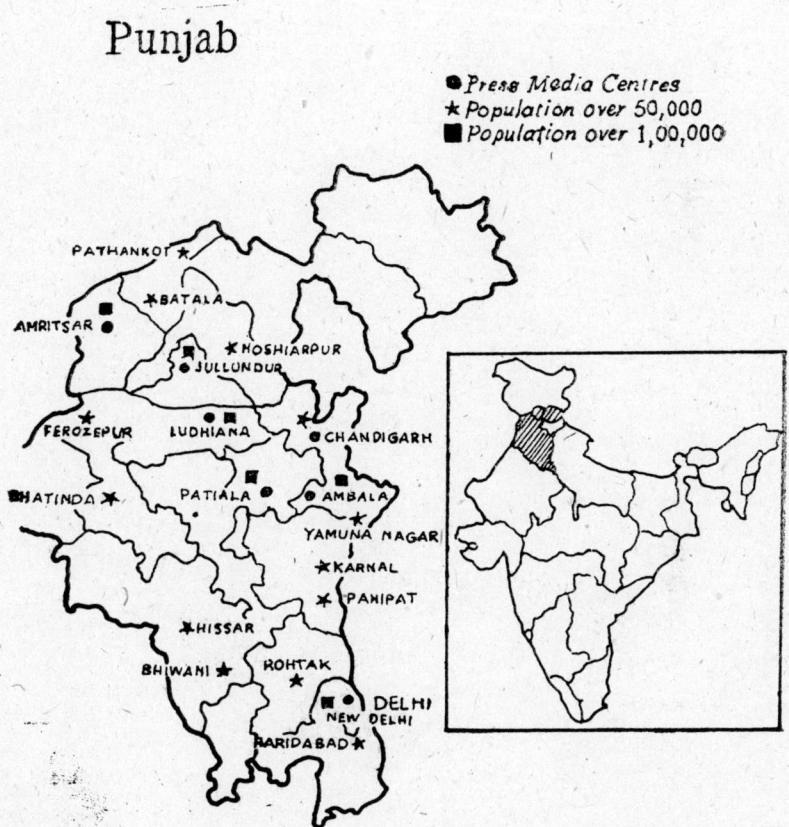

Rajasthan

Appendix A

India

APPENDIX B

SOME BACKGROUND INFORMATION

ACCORDING TO THE CENSUS OF 1961:

1. Total population of India was 439.2 million
   Rural population: 360.3 million
   Urban population: 78.9 million
   Percentage of the rural population to total: 81.99.

2. Literate population was estimated at 24 per cent of the total. Most of it was concentrated in urban areas.

3. Total circulation of all categories of newspapers in 1961, was 4.9 million. Of this, English language papers alone had a circulation of 1.5 million followed by Hindi papers with a circulation of 623,000.

4. DISTRIBUTION OF VILLAGES ACCORDING TO POPULATION (1961)

Population Range	No. of Villages*	Population (Lakhs)
Less than 500	349,568	752.4
500 — 1,000	119,197	838.7
1,000 — 2,000	63,309	894.8
2,000 — 5,000	26,475	764.2
5,000 — 10,000	3,396	221.8
Over 10,000	773	122.5
Total	564,718	3,594.4

*Excluding N.E.F.A. and Goa, Daman & Diu.

Appendix B

NUMBER AND POPULATION OF TOWNS (1961)

Population Range	1961	
	No. of Towns	Population (Lakhs)
Under 5,000	266	80.8
5,000 to 10,000	844	63.1
10,000 to 20,000	817	112.6
20,000 to 50,000	515	156.5
50,000 to 100,000	141	96.3
100,000 to 500,000	95	176.3
500,000 to 1,000,000	5	32.5
Over 1,000,000	7	142.3
Total	2,690	788.4

5. End of 1967, there was 11,678 papers of all categories. Of these 588 were dailies. This meant that there was 1.8 newspaper for 100,000 people. Only three in 100 read a daily paper — 588 papers served 526 million people. An average industrial worker must pay eight days' wages for a years' subscription of an English daily or 6.3 days' wages for a Hindi daily.

6. Papers are concentrated in metropolitan cities (Delhi predominates), state capitals and towns with populations generally of 100,000 or more.

7. A Bengali daily has the largest circulation for any single edition (192,124).

8. English dailies together still command a larger circulation than dailies in any Indian language, including Hindi.

9. At the actual rate of growth of the total circulation of daily newspapers during recent years, circulation is expected to increase at 20 percent a year. It would mean increase of one million a year and quadrupling the circulation over the decade of 1963. Even if it reaches 20 million by 1973, however, it would be reaching less than ten per cent of the total literate population. There would be barely 40 copies per thousand of the population as against 400 per thousand in Japan today.

N.B.: In 1962-63:

The population of Japan was 97,000,000.
Number of households — 22,800,000.
Total national daily circulation — 41,000,000.
Each household subscribed to 1.26 copies of newspapers.

5

THE ECOLOGY OF ART: INDIA AND THE WEST

WALTER M. SPINK

If one looks at the state of culture today in either the east or the west one can find no special cause for hope, to say nothing of celebration. The very fact that we can still speak so easily of "East" and "West" in a world which is rapidly and inexorably developing into what McLuhan has called a "global village" should give us pause. The world's problems are increasingly interconnected, its peoples interdependent. We shall in the end, all suffer and die, or all survive and ultimately dance together.

Our art can tell us much about ourselves, for our productions are, quite literally, the signs of our times, and have always been. And so by evaluating the art of the past and of today, in both east and west, we can get some sense of where we are, where we have been, and even perhaps where we are going.

Art, to state the matter in up-to-date terms, is an ecological phenomenon. It is both a product of, and a factor in, the development of our environment. Like flowers or pollution, it is produced by, but in turn produces our world. We create what we are; we throw off our ideas into form, creating "biographs," pictures and objects by which we come to see and know ourselves. However, in an even deeper sense we *are* what we create; we are described, in a continuing process, by our progeny. The world is an accretion of ideas (among the most potent of which are the ideas embodied in art) even more surely than ideas are an accretion of the world. The Buddha image is as potent as, but a different thing from, the Buddha.

The 1960's may have produced Andy Warhol, but in an even truer sense it was a decade which Andy Warhol produced.

Thus art — the whole spectrum of the productions of the spirit — has profound responsibilities, and is profoundly concerned with the problems of progress, or of escape. We tend, too easily, to think that the scientist dominates the world, when actually his achievements (which we can applaud or condemn, approve or renounce) are only one further signal of our aspirations and our expectations; they are one more sign of our times, which the artist — the moving finger of the public mind — can comment upon and ultimately control.

In neither India nor the United States today, however, does the artist seem very sure of the direction which he, in a very real sense, can discover for his world. Yet there are profound differences in the role which art is playing in these two countries. We can define these differences by placing the artist within the long traditions of culture which he has helped to generate. We shall find, I think, that his role, for all its negative and critical qualities, is a much more healthy and vigorous one in the United States than it is in India, where he has to some degree, (both in city and village) been effected by the stultification — what I shall call the autointoxication — of his tradition.

If we examine what from the critic's point of view is "going on" in the western world and in its heartland (which is undoubtedly the thrusting technological culture of the United States), we find an art and a patronage rooted in the surplus culture which our very advances, at once so full of promise and so full of danger, have produced.

The essence of our art today is essentially materialistic, bereft of those specific religious aspirations which either as a gloss or else very profoundly so many of our past periods have produced. The sea of faith, once at the full, has indeed (in Arnold's words), retreated "down the vast edges drear, and naked shingles of the world."[1] The great mass of our culture here in the United States happily and prosperously accepts those signals of the success of the territorial claims — which,

---

1. From Matthew Arnold, "Dover Beach."

not without difficulty and occasional retreats, we have been striving to achieve ever since that *felix culpa*, that happy and eye-opening fall out of the paradise which god (without consulting us) ordained. The exemplars of this "popular" trend, if two must be picked, are Norman Rockwell, whose heart-warming and assuring pictures still fill so many living rooms in magazines or on the walls; and on a more laudable level, the sensitive and loving recorder of our earthly paradise, Andrew Wyeth — now apparently (and appropriately) the official painter of our president.

But at the frontiers of our art there is — although it may not appear so at first thought — a much more healthy and vigorous questioning of the homely and comforting values which our society has all too readily affirmed. There, in the art of Warhol or Segal or Wesselman or Marisol or Oldenburg, the same material world is seen, but it is seen through a disenchanted eye, roving fingers, and a lashing tongue. In these bitter or bemused or quasiheroic or sardonic revelations of our times, the material world, like a great cancer which may destroy us in the end, is metastasizing, growing strangely huge and soft and deformed. Or else the world is flickering before our eyes like an insistent TV image insistently gone wrong. Things fall apart. The center cannot hold. In Yeats' phrase,[2] the anarchy of excess, the satiations of a land of Cockaigne, "is loosed upon the world" and is viewed, with an already jaundiced eye, as spreading its poisons from within.

These are the pictures of a world and of the values of that world gone wrong; the very images of that lurking fear that our progress, by means of perhaps a slow and polluting or perhaps a sudden and explosive poisoning might mushroom out and ruin us in the end.

And yet the strength of this art — and perhaps this is the strength of western man — is that at its core it is deeply critical. It recognizes — and this recognition extends now into our streets and campuses — that our values have been

---

2. "Things fall apart; the center cannot hold; Mere anarchy is loosed upon the world." From W. B. Yeats: "The Second Coming."

misplaced, and that authority can be questioned. Thus at the core it is an art of hope, for it is an art bent on destroying values which have proved inapplicable to the needs of an increasingly tightening and increasingly frightening world.

It is an art which espouses the same sardonic and far from pretty and (on many levels) far from laudable attitudes as does the "art," the "happenings" created by the mocking Chicago Seven, before the shocked and uncomprehending image of the establishment and the offended god, the Primal Judge. It is an art which, perhaps like the machines of Tinguely, or the silent music of John Cage, is programmed to "self-destruct," to burn the meadow that a greener grass may grow — a dangerous procedure if the forest also catches fire.

Looked at in the context of the intentionally and perversely iconoclastic western tradition, a tradition alternately espousing repression and objection, the contemporary art of our aesthetic frontier becomes clear and even "classic." The imagery, sometimes purely and disturbingly bland, sometimes intensely ironic, resides absolutely in the Here and Now, at the center of the world which man insistently, proudly, and perhaps in desperation — in the face of the erosion of transcendental values — is making, as the inheritor of Adam, for himself.

The history of western art, which cannot be separated from the history of western thought, any more than that of India can be, has always alternated between what I have called elsewhere the poles of dependency and dignity, between those periods when man, determined to assert his ultimate control over his own destiny, has stood proudly (if precariously) upon his own two feet, and those periods when, yielding up his integrity in the face of his fears of Fate and Time and Death, he has fallen to his knees, as subject before king, before an absolute authority above himself, before Jehovah, or before Jove.

The records of the Old Testament and the historical and mythological chronicles of the ancient western world, so different from the chronicles of traditional India, are filled with the stories of what in Freudian terms could be called the primal conflict between father and son, between king and subject, between the creator and his creation, between god and man.[3] One only need think of God's problems with Adam and then with Cain and Jonah and even Job (whose victory was his own); or of Prometheus or Odyssseus; or Christ before the Pharisees; or Socrates, Galileo, or Bobby Seale. Man always loses, ultimately, in these encounters, because the image of authority is by definition beyond disfigurement or death; and man, by definition, is subject to these faults. But in these continuing encounters man constantly tests and criticizes the present and the past and prepares for a new future in which he may, alone, prevail. Thus the western tradition is constantly being cleansed; it is constantly involved in fundamentally traumatic change, in which the excesses of man and the excesses of god are alternately swept away in agonizing reappraisals.

We can see, in a brief survey how this is true.

If we start, for instance, with the images of Periclean Greece, we find man, defining himself (soberly or impetuously) as the "measure of all things", seeing himself as perfectable, heroic self-reliant. "Know thyself," reads the inscription over the shrine of the god at Delphi. "I am beautiful", says an inscription, giving the name of an heroic figure. But this is *hubris* or is ultimately admittedly to be, and man's own image and his possibilities erode before his eyes, as the Hellenic self-reliance plunges with an increasing momentum into the self-deprecations of Hellenistic times and man admits his weakness to his gods.

However the balance swings again. Man reasserts his fragile ego-centered strengths; reduces the stature of his deities, and *Magnum Romanum* is created for its brief bravura hour. But here again the image of man, like the expanse of that great empire which he brought under his control, is eroded in the twilight of that proud day. The Dark Ages, where the only light comes luminously out of the heavens above, not from the radiant mind of man, crept like an engulfing and protecting flood upon the world.

---

3. It is interesting to note that in a recent study, Prof. A. K. Ramanujan finds oedipal conflicts notably lacking in the Hindu epics.

Yet when this inundation (this flood come down from heaven) has receded, the flowers, in gothic fields and songs and underneath the gothic spires, begin to grow again. Man, in a new integrity, as if he were reborn, enters the humanising decades of the Renaissance. Man is again central. God is reduced in his ascendancy and becomes, in Pico della Mirandola's strangely troubling words, merely "a brother to man." Man, in Raphael's *Stanza della Segnatura*, where the very edicts of the church were signed, can stand in the very center of the Vatican, and look around him at a new — a blasphemously balanced — world. Law on one side is equalled by poetry on the other. The disputations of the philosophers — the thoughts of man — are equalled with those of the deity — the thoughts of god.

However, even in the midst of his new assertiveness man's center cannot hold — the center falls apart. Man allows himself, indeed pleads, to be swept up in the spiritualizing maelstroms of mystery and piety of the baroque. But then, with the new rationalism of the Enlightenment, he turns again. At first he reduces these excesses to a human and poetic purpose and then, in a conscious and brutal disruption of grandiloquence and revolt against the artistic and philosophical proprieties of the past, he turns to the purifications of the ordinary, of the world of the here and now, which he soon exalts with an authority-disrupting candor. The past has become passe; so that the art of recent decades is basically an art established in the concerns of the present, its despairs and its delights. Adam and Eve have finally admitted that they were not thrown out of Eden, but that they were born beyond its walls, in a world (to use Camus' phrase) "benignly indifferent" to their fate.[4] "Our exile is ourselves," MacLeish has said.[5] "God is dead" said Nietzesche, and his modern followers are saying the same words.

But if the inceptions of the Hellenic and the Judaeo-Christian culture are based upon a rebellion against authority; if this spirit of criticism, of revolt curiously alternating with respect,

---

4. See A. Camus, "The Stranger."
5. From A. MacLeish, "Eve's Exile."

informs our western world as it changes — and is seen in its secular recensions on our campuses and streets today; if this spirit informs our society and has always informed it with anxiety, it is an anxiety which covets change, which is based upon breaking away from the images of authority and "Truth," rather than upon an ultimate fusion with them. Its expectations are not that self is ultimately Self, but that Self (as god expires) may well be self. That *maya* is not after all *brahman*; but that *brahman* may well, after all, only be *maya*; and that *maya* is not illusion, but reality. That Time is a fact, not a fiction; that Death is not merely part of a cycle, but may well be only one more antagonist which must, with our ways and means, in future time, be overcome. Thus western man, who nearly choked on the apple, may in the end find that it really *will* keep the doctor away.

Our place in the world must, at least presently, still lead to pessimism. Because, as Matthew Arnold despaired:

> "...the world, which seems
> To lie before us like a land of dreams
> So various, so beautiful, so new,
> Hath really neither joy, nor love, nor light,
> Nor certitude, nor peace, nor help for pain;
> And we are here as on a darkling plain
> Swept with confused alarms of struggle and flight,
> Where ignorant armies clash by night."
>
> (from *Dover Beach*)

But Gide says:

> "Look around you. Everything is getting ready for the organization of joy. Behold! All of nature suggests that man is born to be happy. It is the aspiration toward pleasure that provokes the germination of the plant, fills the honeycomb with honey, and man's heart with goodness."
>
> (from *The Fruits of the Earth*)

Does not man ultimately have the potentiality to make the world of work into a world of play? Cannot Eden, in the end, be actuality, if we come to realize that we were never after all *within* it, but from our inception were beyond that womblike, protective, and engulfing place; that we are truly, and have always been, out on our own; that we are standing in the midst of a cosmos that will allow us to control it if we can.

Who cannot seriously believe, seeing the development of technology, that we will not and cannot, within the next few centuries (or, if you will, millenia) conquer Time and Death, and thus reveal the whole supporting miasma of our mythology as a rationalization out of desperation, as a crutch with which we — born in too early an age — limped toward a necessary and inevitable doom. Who cannot believe that it is possible, after these few millenia of walking through the valley of the shadow of death, that we shall not be able to be immortal if we will restructure or rebuild our bodies and the chemical or bioelectrical structure of our souls (the compositions of which we admittedly do not yet understand) at our own or our collective will.

Needless to say, the impact of this apparition of immortality will shake the foundations of our psychological, sociological and political milieu in ways we can hardly today conceive; but this is not a matter with which we can deal with here. Our more immediate problem in the world is to assure that these possibilities, which do indeed "stretch before us as a land of dreams" are not destroyed by the "confused alarms of struggle and flight," and the "ignorant armies" now clashing in the night.[6]

I am no absolute admirer of our western cultural tradition, which is a tradition sponsored by anxiety and compulsion. It may indeed destroy the world in flame, or choke it with emphysema, long before we have the power to truly conquer her and to lie deliciously with her as our gods so long ago so rightly feared we would.[7] It may well have been better — and

6. From Matthew Arnold, "Dover Beach."
7. Genesis III, verses 22, 23: "And the Lord God said, 'Behold, the man is become as one of us, to know good and evil: and now, lest he put forth his hand, and take also of the tree of life, and eat, and live for ever:' Therefore the Lord God sent him forth from the garden of Eden, to till the ground from whence he was taken."

certainly safer — to have seen ourselves as forever circling within the recurrent cosmic processes — to see Time and Death as illusions which in the end overcome themselves, obliterating those anxieties which make of life a desperate race rather than an ever-recurring and fundamentally static dance. "Over the blackened earth" says Yeats, speaking through the "mask" of Mohini Chatterjee...

> "Over the blackened earth,
> The old troops parade.
> Birth is heaped on birth
> That such cannonade
> May thunder time away,
> Birth-hour and death-hour meet.
> Or, as great sages say,
> Men dance on deathless feet"
>
> (from *Mohini Chatterjee*)

Such a view is comforting — indeed it leads to complacency in the face of our apparent Fate — but it has become irrelevant in our coalescing universal culture. Now philosophies come face to face, and the more convincing and therefore stronger, (which to me is the western egocentric view) will surely win — as surely as the tractor and the pill will enter and ultimately destroy the attractive but ultimately irrelevant and un-"modern" form and philosophy of Gandhi's ideal rural world. The critical apostasies of western art will erode — as they are already eroding — the long and beautiful traditions of India's imagery. The latter effect is already to be seen in the second-rate westernized conceptions which so often pass as the art of the elite in India today, or in the third-rate conceptions which are replacing much of the previously vital folk traditions.

The Indian view of man's place in the cosmos, his view of Time and Death and Destiny, is diametrically opposed to that of the west — or at least to that of the Judaeo-Christian tradition which dominates the west. In a superficial sense it posits a similar view for it places man in a world gone wrong, a world which is recognized as a world of death, desire and pain; and this is a world from which man will do well to be released, for as Gautama Buddha said, and as innumerable

Buddhas have said in innumerable world cycles before, *Sabbe sankhara dukkha*, "All is suffering." However this is not because we have been thrown out of Paradise for our effrontery but because Paradise by slow and polluting degrees has been slowly and inexorably receding from us, in the Indian view until, from the *Krta Yuga*, we have reached our present darkening place in time, the *Kali* age.

This world, seen through traditional Indian eyes, is a world which man — although he may (if he can find the solution which the Buddha found) escape it — cannot or need not control; whereas, conversely, man, in the western view, (if he keeps on digging and delving) can perhaps control the earth, but he cannot ever escape it. The primordial Indian ancestor — Manu — was not, as in the western view, suddenly disrupted and on his own; he was not left to his own devices. The traditional Indian is not the grudgingly licenced (or madly unlicensed) driver at the wheel, but is caught upon it as it turns and loses momentum and finally, as it has in all the reduplicated cycles of the past, runs down and stops before — empowered by mysterious forces alien to man — it is set in motion once again.

> "If the red slayer think he slays
> Or if the slain think he is slain
> They know not well the subtle ways
> I keep and pass and turn again."
>
> (Emerson, *Brahma*)

Emerson's unthinking and romantic refrain which in his heart of hearts, being a compulsive and egocentric Harvard man, he did not believe at all, comes directly from the *Upanishads*, where it belongs and was believed profoundly.

Yet in a more perfect day, there was no disruption, no such lack of communication or of identification between the created thing and the creative force. God, in the cool of the day, walked in the garden with the man. That is our western view — before the fall, before that sudden opening of Pandora's box, or of Eve's wedding chest — and before our traumatic and sudden exile to the harsh world East of Eden.

In the various sects of India, a somewhat similar view of an ancient ideal time prevails. In the first and perfect and golden age, according to Jain belief, man did not have to call god forth in revelation, and to seek for him. Man, like Adam before the fall, had never heard of religion (*re-ligio* — to link back or bind); he did not need, because he was *in* yoga (*yuj* — to link).[8] Man in those perfect days entered immediately into identification with the godhead, immediately into salvation, as the end of his span of time on earth. And in this perfect age, as in the *Krta Yuga* of Hindu cosmogony, because the cosmos had not yet become corrupted with its own *karma*, the order of things was remarkably good. The ground itself was sweet as sugar and man enjoyed the gifts of nature for seeming eons. In fact, according to Jain sources, men in that first and best and longest age — which recurs at the start of every cycle — lived ten millions of ten millions of one hundred millions of one hundred million periods of countless years, and were eight miles tall. Such men had 256 ribs, as opposed to the 16 which according to Jain physiology we have today.[9]

But now we know, here on this darkling plane, here in a Brindaban constantly assaulted by disordering demonic forces, that the soil is bitter to the taste and that the world, when it reveals its inmost and most true faces to us, "hath really neither joy, nor love, nor light, nor certitude, nor peace, nor help for pain." The reason is clear. We are, by an unfortunate but nonetheless irrevocable happenstance of fate, living in the *Kali Yuga;* or according to Jain chronology, in the increasingly bad fifth of the six ages which comprise the cosmos' declining cycles — an age which on a normal university marking scale would receive approximately D minus.

This absorption of man in the engulfing and irresistible wheel (web) of process involves him fundamentally and at the psychic level — within the coercion of circumstance. He is, and the world is, what he and it must be for there is fundamentally no free will, no choice. The result tends to be an attitude of complacency — quite opposed to the western attitude of anxiety. There is, inevitably, less questioning of values, less assertion

8. For a discussion of Jain beliefs, see J. Campbell, *The Masks of God: Oriental Mythology*, New York, 1962, Chapter 4.
9. Idem.

of the need for or the right to change. In a much more subtle way than in the west the establishment prevails: The individual, instead of being exposed to and in conflict with the establishment is, in the preordained and hierarchical scheme of things, a part of the establishment itself. Man should be what he is, not what he might become. Why else should Arjuna, to do his duty, kill his kin and help decide the outcome of a battle whose origins and endings were both predestined from the start. Why else should the god dance into conflict with the demonic forces of the world when in these already resolved encounters the demons always lose.

The Indian tradition is, at its base, essentially uncritical of its values. It adds to but it does not negate them. It does not cleanse itself, as does the troubled western tradition, of its accretions. The Indian tradition supports and in this sense approves (even if it does not sponsor) the pessimistic and fundamentally uncritical or uncriticized cosmological view which we have outlined above. The gods come to save the world but they must come with increasing frequency; and they are increasingly powerless to change the weakening and wheeling cycles of decline. The cow of *dharma* who in the *Krita Yuga* stood so stably on four legs now balances — one can imagine how precariously — on only one. There is no food, no *suddhayajna* which can keep her from toppling back into the primordial ocean in the end.

The history of Indian art is a remarkable history of the resistance to change. It is the history of the constant reassertion of established standards, of a growth around a central core of ideas which tend always to be retained even if they are adjusted. There is never a traumatic shift of values and of forms such as one finds in the west, except under the direct impact of other influences. The "little traditions", which in every culture are the conflicting and confronting — the threatening — traditions, never finally triumph but in the end are always absorbed into the "great tradition" according to a pragmatic system of identification. They assert, if the question be raised, that *tat twam asi*, "that art thou" — that the Buddha, or Jagannath, (who *is* Krishna), or Krishna (who *is* Vishnu) is, after all, no other than Shiva, and indeed that Shiva is no other than the Self. This process of exclusion by inclusion, of a subtle ideological gamesmanship, deadens conflict and change. It causes the cohesion of belief, supported by the cohesion of forms, around a single central core. Quite in contrast, western man could never (nor would ever) admit that he and the Lord (at least in essence) are One. He would at best (and from the deity's standpoint, shockingly) cast God or the gods in his own image, further asserting his egocentricity. Thus Gauguin can see himself as Christ and paint Christ as himself, for Christs's sufferings have become his metaphor. Simonetta Vespucci can pose quite proudly as Venus, the erotic muse, because, (at least when we are feeling most assertive) we measure God or the gods in man's dimensions and in his forms.

How different is the case in India, where with an ego-dissolving and time-dissolving insistence the ideal queen in any age is portrayed not as herself but as Laksmi, the auspicious goddess, and the hero or the king is figured (and in the literature described) not in his own ephemeral guise but in the generalized and perfected lineaments of Vishnu or of Shiva, who themselves are only revelations of a perfection not to be found in the world of place and time. History dissolves into theology, time into the timeless. The many become the One.

This inherent resistance to change — this rather Platonic, certainly not Aristotelean, notion — that things which are manifest are only imperfect reflection of ephemeral revelations of eternal and established Forms, that the earth is the earth come down from Heaven, that man may continually define but not destroy these truths — constricts the development of Indian social and artistic growth, and at the same time constructs it. Norm and form develop in parallel instead of in continual or at least potential opposition. The ideal — and this can still be seen affecting (I would say adversely) Indian education today — is for the student to confirm rather than to question the teacher or the tradition. This is a very different attitude from the western view that the student (at least if he does it with a certain tact) will be a superior student if he proves his teacher wrong. The only Doubting Thomases in the Indian tradition are demons, not devotees; and the demons of course are all coverted (if they are not destroyed) in the end. This goes without saying; because it was said *in illo tempo* when the unmanifest said "bhuh" and the manifest was made.

When we survey the development of Indian art we do not, as in the west, see a continual alternation of ideas and the motifs expressive and productive of them, but a continual accumulation and accretion, elaboration and ornamentation, addition rather than disruption, around a central core. This often leads to intricate marvels of enriched meaning, but the threat of surfeit, of autointoxication (rather than catharsis) is also always there. Change, instead of taking place by negation and by criticism takes place through augmentation. The authority of the Vedas is never questioned but is elaborated upon, and sometimes inundated beneath a flood of commentaries and of commentaries upon those commentaries. In this process it is true that certain original intentions and early gods may drown or suffocate, while others prosper. But the original truth remains unquestioned because, in a quite different sense from that intended by Gertrude Stein upon her death-bed, there is ultimately no question to ask; indeed there is no one to ask it of.

Indian music, to consider another sphere of art, becomes (melodically and rhythmically) increasingly more complex whether we are speaking of the performance of a single piece or of the development of its long tradition. In the latter, the *ragas* add to their store of concubines (raginis) until the landscape is crowded with their presences. But there are stories of these beautiful creatures writhing in agony upon the floors of the celestial palaces in which they are embodied, when musicians here on earth have knowingly or unknowingly destroyed the established patterns in which they are made manifest in rhythm and in sound.

The kind of skillful ornamentation and complication found in the display of the Indian *ragas* is akin to the manner in which the Vedas will (by the elect and the adept) be learned by rote, syllable by endless syllable, and repeated with an exactitude which has allowed no change, century after century; or the syllables, still subservient to the central core of **form** (if not of apparent meaning) may be recited backwards or in a great number of strict canonical variations.

Indian poetry and epic prose is treated with a similar elaborateness as it develops. In certain styles of the early medieval period a tremendous emphasis is placed on elaborated puns. Sometimes whole sentences can be read with continual dual meanings, while the use of metaphor proliferates to such a degree that certain common words — for instance, horse or maiden — can be expressed in literally hundreds of varying ways, the end result being a prose style marvelously encrusted with ornament, marvelously burdened with excess. At other times the poet, with almost incredible shows of *tour-de-force*, will create whole stanzas using only a single consonant; stanzas which can be read in exactly the same way from start to finish, or from finish to start, or other startlingly academic stanzaic forms. Basham has quoted a few notable examples.[10]

Ekaksara (employing only one consonant throughout)

Dadado dudda-dud-dadi dadado duda-di-da-doh dud-dudam dadade dudde dad'-adada-dado' da-dah.	The giver of gifts, the giver of grief to his foes, the bestower of purity, whose arm destroys the givers of grief, the destroyer of demons, bestower of bounty on generous and miser alike, raised his weapon against the foe.

Sarvatobhadra (mixed syllabic palindrome and acrostic)

Sakara-nan 'ara-kasa-kaya-sada-da-sayaka ras'-ahava vaha-sara nadavada-da-vadana.	His army was eager for battle, whose arrows destroyed the bodies of the varied hosts of his brave enemies. Its trumpets vied with the cries of the splendid horses and elephants.

Gatapratyagatam ("gone and come back," a perfect syllabic palindrome)

Tam Sriya ghanaya 'nasta-ruca sarataya taya yataya tarasa caru-stanaya 'naghay' asritam.	He who was eagerly and closely embraced by the fair-bosomed Sri, the sinless goddess, of never-failing beauty, and endowed, with every excellence.

10. A. L. Basham. *The Wonder that was India*. New York, 1954, pp. 423-424.

Even in the realm of erotics, the simpler and more fluid recipes of the *Kamasutra* become increasingly elaborated and categorized in such later works as the *Kokasastra*, which is much more a prosaically outlined catalog of the types of women and organs and pinches and poses than an aesthetic travelogue for the man about town.

The caste system too, which began in the centuries B.C. in a rather pragmatic way became increasingly refined and defined, radiating out by the medieval period into what had become an oppressive but highly controlled jungle of categorization, sanctified by the establishment and subject to any truly disruptive changes only in exceptional circumstances. Even Gandhi, with his own moral force and the force of much untraditional opinion to support him, could not escape this realization. Why else, when after the *harijans* in one town had tried out their new constitutional rights and gone to worship at a temple previously excluded from them, did the gods burn their village down that very night? Why else, in certain converted communities, do men still speak of Brahmin Christians and Vaisya Christians and look with a real even if perhaps somewhat guilty disfavor on intermarriage between such groups?

If we follow the development of Indian imagery we find a similar process taking place. The old brahmanical tradition was extremely resistant to depicting the god in anthropomorphic form, and indeed this would never have been accomplished were it not for pressures external to this central — what we can call the Great — tradition. It was in Buddhism and Jainism — which it is important to note were never truly revolts against but more truly reformations or variations of this Great Tradition — that it was accomplished, and it was accomplished due to the impact of foreign influence and of influences from lesser autochthonous cults. Thus in early Buddhism and Jainism (say before the first century A.D.) the Buddha and the Jain are never shown in human form. This is due to proscriptions which can be traced back through the Aryans to Persia and to the iconoclastic traditions of the world of the Semites and of the ancestral Indo-Europeans. But in Buddhist and Jain contexts, partly due to the influx of peoples and ideas from the image oriented Graeco-Roman world, it became acceptable and indeed customary to represent lesser divinities — *nagas* and *yakshas* and even the brahmanical gods such as Indra and Brahma — as servitors. Thus the spark was lit.

Once these inroads against the creation of images were made, the Buddha and the Jain too, due (as we might say) to popular demand, were represented in human guise. Then the concomitantly developing Hindu cults, notably the Shaivite and Vaisnavite cults as if to "keep up with the times", allowed the representation of their cult divinities, too. The first few centuries of the Christian era were centuries of formulation, of a conquest of the technical and conceptual problems of casting such images in appropriately ideal lineaments. By the Gupta period, remarkable for its developments in every sphere under an exuberant and discriminating patronage, a canon of form had been developed which could be called an ideal vessel to contain the imagery — the form of the *mahapurusa*.

Once this form was found it was, quite typically for India's highly traditional and authoritarian culture, fixed. All later imagery measures itself to some degree against the canons established at this time. One could say that the core idea — or ideal — never changes (as it *does*, for instance in the west when we move from the Greek conception of the god or of man to that of the Middle Ages). All later imagery — and this could also be said of the imagery of literature and of society — is fundamentally only a variation on an elaboration of, and an augmentation of, this theme. Tradition takes over, and the artist, as the philosopher, the king, and the common man, is its servitor.

The dangers in such a situation are manifest, for where there is an innate resistance to change, there is the constant danger of stultification, of forms ingrowing or proliferating in outgrowths upon themselves. And just as the Vedas cannot be violated, and just as the *ragas* and *raginis* must not be hurt by the predilections of the performer, it became — or so said the letter of the law — essential that the absolute prescriptions for the image be retained. The *sastras* — the rule books which guide the artist, who is really conceived as a craftsman in the service of the established order — are full of rules and warnings:

> "The deficiency in the length and breadth of an image causes famine and revolution. If it be deficient in body, its maker or donor becomes hunchbacked and if it be noseless then he gets ill. The eyesight of an image turned towards the left destroys one's fame, while the same raised upwards causes loss of wealth,... If the image is made with a sunken belly there will always be destruction of crops; if its thighs be less in measurement then abortion will certainly be caused..."[11]

And yet of course the forms *do* change: pressing internal and external forces which affect any given culture at any given time break down or alter these proscriptions. The threatening texts are trying to hold back the tide of an inevitable and understandable growth. Clearly they are overstatements, but they do have this effect: namely, that all things continue to adhere to tradition's assertive and established core. The changes are gradual; there are never the dramatic, diametrical, and even dangerous shifts which the constantly ambivalent western tradition sees, in retrospect, as *its* norm.

In architecture, for instance, we never move, as in the west, from spires to domes, from seeking and beseeching to self-centered and containing forms. No two Indian temples are the same, but they all have essentially related meanings and essentially connected forms. Movement is gradual from the rudimentary towers of the Gupta and early medieval periods to the fantastically elaborate and technically remarkable soaring *sikharas* of the later centuries. Similarly, one could show a gradual and persistent growth from the simple Buddhist *stupas* of the Sunga period to their later recensions throughout India itself or in the far Southeast Asian lands to which the Indian tradition moved. In the same way we move from altars with a single Buddha — invariable before the fifth century — to increasingly complicated groups of two or four or many

---

11. See J. N. Banerjee, *The Development of Hindu Iconography*, (2nd edition, Calcutta, 1956), p. 610.

more, or to the unquenchable revelations of imagery — all still cohering around a single source and ultimately reducible to a single unity — in the later Mahayana paradises and in the proliferating *mandalas* of Tibet and of other Asian lands. We move from the single and monumental images of Shiva found in the sixth century at Elephanta, to the inexhaustibly innumerable names and forms of this same or other (but ultimately identical) god on the oppressively ornamented towers of later India.

The aesthetic and perhaps even ideological dangers in such a situation spring easily to mind, for quantity rather than quality can all too easily become the rule: a thousand insignificant arms can replace two beautiful and potent ones. A great Tibetan prayer wheel, shaped and sized like a barrel, stuffed with literally thousands of tiny incantations (*om mane padme hum*) inscribed on slips of paper — the whole powered by a windmill to make it spin can all too easily replace a single heartfelt incantation or circumambulation. Methods and materials — the panoplies of ritual — metastacize, even though the meaning, reduced and then multiplied again by such redundancy, remains in the ultimate analysis the same. One merely has to run harder to stand at the *still point*: to dance more wildly (and perhaps less decorously) to find the ultimate calm. Autointoxication and enervation, the rule of excess, can set in. The forest can be lost for the trees, the central trunk hid by its accumulating branches and its clogging roots.

Thus there is a tendency for Indian art, because of the authoritarian prescriptions placed upon it, to become ingrown. It moves, as it were, from its own *Krta Yuga* to its predestined and declining *Kali* Age. And this is true not *only* of the artistic tradition; the possibilities of catharsis, of a sweeping away and a cleansing of used and enervating forms and ideas is largely disallowed by the hieratic structures of the entire culture.

But this is perhaps too negative a picture. For if western art and culture achieves its potency from the exciting and dangerous shifts and ruptures in its radition of *dichotomy*, the ancient values of Indian culture have often reaffirmed their potency within the tradition of *unity*. In such periods, however, artists never actually broke away from but instead marvelously enriched and reinvigorated the basic form and content of their tradition. It is certainly significant that these periods were nearly always moments of dynastic patronage, inspired by pious as well as political factors. The inspiring temple complexes of Khajuraho or of Orissa or of Tanjore or of Mysore or of many other regions still stand as evidence.

The last truly great expression of the Indian artistic tradition — or at least of the total dominance of the Great Tradition — can be seen in the realm of painting, specifically in the productions of the courts of Rajputana and of the Pahari region in the seventeenth and eighteenth centuries. Paradoxically, this era of significant effort was founded to some degree upon the new directions sponsored by the impact of Persian and European influences during the heyday of the Mughals and their immediate precursors. Their disruptive advances broke the stultifying traditions into which painting had moved by the fifteenth century and a new energy effected the courts which, directly or indirectly, were under their influence. But the Mughals understood and appreciated and ultimately were largely absorbed into the Indian context which they invaded and effected. India was still somewhat insulated from continuing external impacts. Brindaban still really *could* be considered as a microcosmic reflection of the larger reality. The art of the Rajput courts reflects a way of thought filled with conviction, still unquestioning of ancient values, or customs.

But such an art — as we can see when we move into the nineteenth century — could not survive the onslaughts of the intensifying foreign domination which came with the English rule. It retreated to the village and to the forest, in an India which with its developing systems of communication and centralization was becoming a more and more un-Indian land, in at least the old traditional sense.

India is moving now, for better or for worse, inevitably into a *mariage de convenance* with the world outside of itself; and that outer world is a world which I think it is fair to say will affect, more than it is affected by, traditional Indian forms and values.

When we turn to a consideration of Indian art in the present day, the picture which we see is not an encouraging one. If the art of the west seems at present goal-less, critical of the present but unsure of the future, the art of India today seems to be in an equally difficult state. Indeed, it lacks the self-critical quality which may in the end lead western art into a new resolution.

The situation of the visual arts in India today directly reflects and typifies the difficulties of India's whole cultural situation, caught between its rich and still-demanding past, and an inevitably very different future. There is no single mode which could be called an art for the masses in India today, for its art divides, very roughly, into two broad categories — one of indigenous and one of foreign origin.

I shall not discuss here the latter category — namely the actively developing but by and large still weakly eclectic productions of recent and contemporary painters and sculptors attracted by the conventions of modern (or earlier) western art. Such art is often charming and colourful and craftsmanly, but it is an art produced by and for an elite to whom its deeper levels of both form and content are still too alien to ring with any arresting authority. Perhaps it is fair to say that it is an art which, in the midst of the great developmental problems which face India today, is essentially not needed; at least it is not being called forth by the kind of totally committed and demanding patronage which for pious or public purposes urged such remarkable and relevant creations out of India's artists in many of the periods of the past.

In a way the pretty and often excessively voluptuous popular poster art which floods the stores and bazaars of India today is a more relevant and even more vital kind of production. In a curious way it bridges the gap between India and the west. Of course it seems marvelously "camp" to the western eye bemused by such highly sentimentalized and "realistic" religious productions. However, before we dismiss such excesses with too quick a smile, we should remember that this art — via the English impact on India — comes straight out of our grandparents' Pre-Raphaelite dreamworld, and continues its hold on the less sophisticated segments of our own society today too. The problem with such art in India, is that in satisfying the public need for assurance of the tangible presence of the popular gods it threatens the more truly indigenous folk tradition.

This folk tradition, although still strong in certain areas, is encountering extreme difficulties. It is by and large the art of village India and is sponsored by a strong religious urgency. Generally it is an art without pretentions, created by anonymous craftsmen, or often by the women of the village, to enliven life with colour and with form, to praise or else coerce the numerous gods, or to ward off threatening presences.

Such art — delightful in its vigor and its conviction to our modern eyes — is still produced in abundance in India today; but it is threatened by external forces which, almost inevitably, must ultimately spell its doom. With the advent of increasing modes of communication between village and city, and between the cities and the western world, the work of these artists is threatened by the influx of the sentimentalized creations of which we spoke above. The latter, done in the commercial press, compete in availability and cost with these remnants of the country's long traditions. And unfortunately the eye of the villager is all too easily coerced by the slick "realistic" forms just as the attractions of a communal radio (or in the days to come, TV) can also easily destroy involvement in the local traditions of dance and song and story. Under such onslaughts from without, ancient traditions rapidly decline.

A case in point known to me personally involve the flooding of the pilgrimage center of Puri, the locale of the famous annual Jagannath festival, with cheap and glistening chromo-lithographs of that favorite local deity and of associated gods.[12] When this influx began, only a few decades ago, the painters in the villages nearby, who for centuries had been supplying paintings for temples and travellers alike, were suddenly in acute financial jeopardy as their means of livelihood rapidly

12. See W. Spark, "Indian Folk Art: Orissan Painting" in *Institute of International Education News Bulletin,* December 1953, pp. 15-19; 36.

was eroded. Their desperation was further exacerbated by the problems of caste and occupational restrictions, for neither were they trained for nor allowed to enter most other occupations. Forced to compete or starve, these families of painters and sculptors, whose forefathers had created the great temples of the Orissan style at Bhubanesvara, Konarak, Puri, and other sites, had to lower the standards of their already declining art. They quite literally had to do more work faster and to sell it cheaper. Even so their situation went from bad to worse.

Fortunately — or perhaps not — a partial solution was in sight, for a concerned local resident,[13] aided in fact by the governor of Orissa himself, recognized the interest which these art forms could have for a wider audience. She managed to assure the survival of both the artists and the art by finding an outlet for it along with the splendid hand-loomed fabrics of the region in government sponsored, cottage industries emporia in some of the major cities of the country, and eventually also abroad. But as one can imagine the new "patronage" was one interested merely in the charm, the emptying forms of the art, and not in its older and profound significance. The paintings became, as it were, examples of folk-crafts for tourists instead of art-offerings for pious pilgrims or for the powerful gods.

The artists could now "afford" to take more time and create more careful and elaborate images, since their market was now no longer comprised of poor pilgrims but of the wealthy urban or foreign class. In some ways quality was improved; but at the same time the deeper inspiration of the artists yielded to (or was compromised by) the demands and desires of the merchandisers, who were far less concerned about the potency of the images than by the profits to be made. The artists now also started to produce skillful but "insignificant" copies of the great sculptures of the temples of the region. They have been commercialized; they work for the Delhi market, or the markets of New York, and although they still work with energy, they no longer need to work with divine inspiration, since this motive is not essential to production.

13. The lady to whom much credit is due is Mrs. Helena Zealey.

Something of the same debilitating effect can be seen in the production of hand-woven textiles in many parts of India today, where production is no longer by the piece but by the bolt. The patterns, made to be cut up by the dressmakers of some distant urban market, are no longer allowed to vary, with their ancient freshness, from the production norms.

Asok Mitra, one of the most intelligent and dedicated people concerned with the problems of preserving the vitality of India's folk arts, has lamented these problems, noting that "it seems that if a thing is deprived of its function it is deprived of its character and starts to crumble." Indeed, he points out, "face to face with (this) new situation, the village artist degenerates (just) as so many tribes preternaturally decay at the first contact with civilisation." He suggests that "It is well to concede the fact that a country whose internal economy still depends so much on its own handicraft can hardly afford to look in a big way at the export market, especially when the object of handicraft promotion is still primarily to increase internal circulation... It is well to realise that a handicraft developed exclusively for export quickly degenerates into arty-craftness. It is odd to think of a culture which a nation develops, not for its own use, but for export..." Therefore, he concludes, when one considers what is actually "the very little proportion (Indian) handicrafts earn in relation to our total foreign exchange earnings... export of handicraft should ... be (he feels) of very minor consequence to a country's trade policy, unless it is bent on destroying traditions."[14]

But I fear that, even though one might indeed do much to preserve the vitality of these traditions, isolating them from the demands of the market would mean insulating village India from the modern world. Such a policy, considering the development of communications and all of the other pressures of an invading technological counter-culture, is quite unrealistic. Mulk Raj Anand's pessimistic prediction is, I am afraid, much more to the point, namely, "that the impact of the industrial revolution will ultimately envelop the whole of the Indian people," and that all we can hope for is "that for a

---

14. *Marg*, Vol. XXII, number 4 (September 1969), pp. 58-60.

hundred years or so, it is likely that in the rural civilisation, the art expression will (at least here and there) remain."

This is of course essentially an admission of the hopelessness of the situation, but it is a realistic view. A new and changing culture will without any question eventually engulf village India and sweep away these now still meaningful remnants of traditional culture, as surely as the motorcar in America has replaced the horse, and the mechanic, the blacksmith. Gandhi's dream of perpetuating a closed and largely self-sufficient village society, allowing only a limited and carefully controlled use of the machine, was, I think it is fair to say, a plan doomed to failure from the start. As Anand points out, "nowhere in the whole world has the industrial society allowed the rural mass to remain outside the orbit of its economic domination."

If these changes are bound to come; if as it seems to me the ideologies and the aspirations of the western world are destined (whether we would wish it or not) to triumph in the end, then our ultimate concern must be that the ideological values of western culture, which at present do not seem adequate to secure a safe and happy future, must be tempered by the values of the less compulsive and egocentric Indian philosophy. Similarly, the literature, art, music and dance of India should help to transform and enrich culture in the west and to fuse with them to form the thoughts and actions of a single and unified world dominated neither by God nor by the gods but by a changing and improving and perhaps ultimately perfectible man.

It is not likely that man, now that even the moon is in his grasp, is going to give up the world of *maya* for the void of *brahman* — even if some would insist that this void is actually a plenum. Nor do we feel he should; for the world of *maya* may not turn out to be mere illusion after all; and the apocalpse too may never descend in all its awesomeness, upon us. Both the western view of religion and the eastern view will certainly (if we survive) prove to be rationalizations out of desperation, merely figments of the imagination of an exiled Adam caught in the *Kali* Age. The day of the global village is bound to come. Man, from his present primitive state, can certainly — even if it does not arrive for many generations hence — prepare himself for the day when the Buddha's assumption that "all is suffering" and Jehovah's prediction that all men are doomed to external judgment and to death will both seem—to our fortunate progeny irrelevant and quaint comment out of man's pained and brutal past.[15]

15. It might be noted that this paper, as originally presented in lecture form, was illustrated with approximately one hundred slides. The reader's indulgence is requested, since it has not been feasible to illustrate it in its present published form.

6

MUSIC AND MASS CULTURE IN INDIA

MAHADEV L. APTE

As a prerequisite to a discussion of the relationship between music and mass culture in India, it is necessary to define the concept of mass culture in the Indian context and to explain which types of music are to be included.

Redfield has pointed out[1] that the difference between a civilization and a culture is in the division of labor, existence of surplus food, and the presence of a group which does not participate in the productive process, but is engaged in the control and distribution of goods. This small minority "administers" the various activities of the society in general; and provides the peace and stability needed for the masses to engage in production. It is usually called the gentry, and at their head is a king, who symbolizes their control.

Before industrialization, the gap between the various strata of society was considerable. While the majority were involved in production activities, especially of food and other basic necessities, the minority in control created entertainment which was sophisticated, complex, and therefore alien to the rest of society, both in terms of participation and appreciation. Needless to say, such a social structure led to the hierarchical system in which those at the top began to consider themselves and were considered by others as "elites."

Kroeber's definition of culture as "the mass of learned and transmitted motor reactions, habits, techniques, ideas and

---

1. R. Redifield, "Thinking about a Civilization," in M. Singer ed. *Introducing India in Liberal Education,* Chicago, 1957, pp. 3-15.

values — and the behaviour they induce",[2] is generally accepted by anthropologists, although there may be disagreements about the exact wording, and the marginal status of some aspects — for example the question of whether arts and artifacts are to be considered as part of the culture. In any case, culture, as understood in this sense, encompasses all segments of a society, although depending on the size and the historical development, a society may be composed of several "sub-cultures." This concept of culture automatically includes the masses; it may be labelled *Culture 1*.

As generally used in both the western and eastern worlds, especially in countries that have a long history of civilization, "culture" has quite a different connotation. It usually means familiarity with and knowledge of the creations of professional artists, which only the elites appreciate and enjoy. The arts, which include painting, music, sculpture, and literature, generally form the major content of culture in this sense; thus a "cultured" individual is one who appreciates the arts and enjoys them, and can talk about them in a sophisticated manner. Such sophistication generally includes an intellectual rationalization of the process of enjoyment, which in turn is dependent on the critical evaluation of the art object itself.[3] As a result of this phenomenon, there are always those among the elites who make it their profession to be "culture brokers" and provide readymade intellectual analyses. Cultured individuals are expected to appreciate such analyses and to evaluate for themselves the varying opinions of the experts. This art, and its appreciation by the elites, with the intellectual rationalization of the pleasure gained from it, may be labelled *Culture 2*.

The growth of technology, education, and an abundance of leisure time, has created a demand for *Culture 2* by the majority, who until recently were not in a position to enjoy it, either because of their preoccupation with daily survival, or their feelings of inadequacy in the elite's domain. This is not to say that the masses did not have their own forms of entertainment. However, the structure of such art was relatively

---

2. A. L. Kroeber, *Anthropology*, New York, 1948.
3. L. Rosten, "The Intellectual and the Mass Media," in *Daedalus*, Vol. 89, No. 2, 1960, pp. 334 ff.

simple, and usually associated with religious beliefs and customs; the idea of entertainment purely for the sake of enjoyment was not as strong as it was in *Culture 2*. Such forms of art are labelled by the elites as "folk" art.

In the process of the popularization of *Culture 2*, there is the possibility that the elite culture will be exposed to dilution and simplification. The experts generally think that this is an inevitable process,[4] since the ratio of quality to quantity is always inverse. Alternatively, there is the possibility of elevating the general level of education and sophistication to the degree where *Culture 2* can be "truly" appreciated. The result of such efforts is what is commonly labelled as "popular" culture — a culture which is neither "classical," as is *Culture 2*, nor stable, as is "folk" culture. Popular culture thrives on the demands of the masses and turns and twists according to their whims, acceptance, and rejection.[5]

Music, as the term is generally used, is any patterned expression of tones and tunes through the medium of the human voice, or through any man-made instrument. Human beings often perceive consonance in the verbal expression of animals, especially birds, and in the various sounds in nature. To be considered as music, these sounds must be recreated by the media above.

Music, like other arts, reflects the basic emotions of individuals and groups. It is closely related to many aspects of culture. "In music, as in the other arts, basic attitudes, sanctions, and the values are often stripped to their essentials; music is also symbolic in some ways, and it reflects the organization of society."[6] The existence of music in culture is universal; every culture has music, be it verbal, or instrumental. However, music cannot be removed from the particular culture in which it was developed. The common misconception about music, and the other arts, is that it can be understood universally, and that there are no cultural barriers to its enjoyment.

---

4. Stanley Hyman, "Ideals, Dangers and Limitations of Mass Culture," and E. Van Den Haag, "A Dissent from the Consensual Society," *Daedalus*, Vol. 89, No. 2, 1960, pp. 317, 381.

5. Van Den Haag, op. cit., pp. 318-19.

6. Alan P. Merriam, *The Anthropology of Music*, 1964, p. 13.

Music, following this logic, is often contrasted with language, which may be considered the biggest obstacle in understanding other cultures. This supposition is only partly true. Music is used as a means of self-expression in all cultures, and in that sense it is universal. However, music is very much the part of the totality which we labelled *Culture 1*, and it cannot be appreciated, evaluated, or analyzed out of its own context. Barriers to the appreciation of music of different cultures must exist, since with all artistic creations, individuals automatically and unconsciously relate the artistic form to their own experience. It is only natural for them to view and appreciate the artistic expressions of other cultures from the same point of view.

Some ethnomusicologists argue that people in the western world tend to think of music as culture-free because the concept of culture has been bifurcated — the distinction made above between *Culture 1* and *Culture 2* — so that "culture is often understood in the sense of 'cultivated,' with a particular emphasis on art forms and art for art's sake." The result of this cultural trait of ours has been a separation of art from culture-as-a-whole. "We are more likely to discuss the creative periods of Picasso than Picasso as a manifestation of the social, religious and economic pressures of his times, or in other words, Picasso as a manifestation of his culture."[7] This is also the case with music, where "we are most likely to discuss a song as an art form, as pretty or ugly and why, and in many other ways outside its principal cultural function."[8] Ethnomusicologists consider that it is just as important to study the interrelationship between music and culture as it is to study music as an art form. Music can be best understood as an art form once it has been correlated with the culture from which it springs, since such correlation explains at least in part the symbolism involved and the particular mode of expression.

Before considering the significance of music in the mass culture of India, it is necessary to present some background infor-

---

7. David McAllester, "The role of music in Western Apache culture," in Anthony F. C. Wallace ed. *Selected Papers of the Fifth International Congress of Anthropological and Ethnological Sciences,* 1960, p. 468.
8. Ibid.

mation about Indian music, both from the historical[9] and the contemporary point of view.

The recorded history of music in India goes back to the Vedic period which is conservatively estimated to have begun around 1500 B.C. Sama Veda, one of the four original Vedas, is generally considered as the source of Indian music.[10] In fact, many portions of the Sama Veda are portions from the Rig Veda, rearranged or expanded to facilitate its singing. The development of music in India during that period is closely related to the religious rituals in which the religious texts were recited in a particular manner with emphasis on the proper syllables and with high and low notes on certain syllables. This tradition of recitation of the Veda is still maintained in many parts of India.[11] The claim is made that even before the end of the Vedic period the scale of seven notes, so basic a concept in the classical music of India, was completed, and that all the tempos of the rhythms were known in the later Vedic Age. At the beginning these rhythms had only three time units.

Most of the recitation of the early Vedic period was liturgical and it was only during the classical Sanskrit period that music was recognized as secular. Just before the beginning of the classical period, a distinction was evolving, namely the *Marga* (sought after) music, and the *Desi* (of the region) music. It is likely that even during the Vedic period, the Aryans probably adopted the folk music of the various regions and tribes of India. Early during the classical period, the *Marga* music was sung by professional singers called *Gandharvas* and therefore came to be called *Gandharva* music. In Indian mythology, *Gandharva* is a singer and is assigned the status of semigod. He was supposed to be a wanderer. It is likely that the term came from the regional name *Gandhar Desa*, which is the modern Kandahar and its outlying regions, and which also

---

9. The information given in this and following five paragraphs is based on the following sources: O. Gosvami, *The Story of Indian Music*, New York, 1957, and V. Agarwala, *Traditions and Trends in Indian Music*, Meerut, India, 1966.

10. A. L. Basham, *The Wonder that was India*, New York, 1954, p. 382.

11. J. F. Staal, *Nambudiri Veda Recitation*, 'S-Gravenhage, 1961.

gave to India at a later date the sculptural art known as *Gandhara* art.

By the third or fourth century A.D. the Indians had established the difference between *sruti* (a note of minute pitch which the ear is capable of hearing) and *svara* (the sound that generates an expression) and had discovered that separate pitches cannot be heard unless there is a minimum interval between them, and that when the successive pitches having this minimum interval were counted they numbered twenty-two in an octave. The famous treatise of Bharata, the *Natya Sastra* which dealt with dramaturgy and treated music only incidently is the only source through which the state of music around the third century A.D. is known. Besides the flute, the Veena was being accepted as an accompanying instrument, and music was sung on the basic scale of the Veena which comprised seven notes. Bharata comments on the various combinations of ascending and descending tones which he calls *jati*. The term *raga* was used by Matanga in his text *Brihaddesi* which dealt with indigenous music. He defines raga as "a combination of attractive notes which, with beautiful illuminating graces, please the people in general." He compiled a list of *ragas* that were contributed by the non-Aryan tribes to Aryan music.

The development of classical music in India thus shows a continuum through the post-classical period during which the basic divisions of the tunes were maintained and many *ragas* were composed. However, little is available after Bharata and before the major treatise by Sarangadeva called *Sangita Ratnakara*, literally, "the sea of the music pearls," was composed in the thirteenth century. This treatise influenced the development of music in Northern India for the next five hundred years. Although many well-known singers and musicians during the Mughal period are credited with the creation of new *ragas*, it was not until the early nineteenth century that a reclassification of the *ragas* into ten main scales called the *That* took place. This new method was further popularized by Pandit Bhatkhande. Each of these ten scales was named after its first *raga*, and many new *ragas* can be generated by the application of the laws of *raga*-construction.

Although it is generally accepted that there are two major

types of Indian music, 1) the North Indian classical music and 2) the South Indian or Carnatic music, it is postulated that both had a common origin and did not bifurcate into separate systems until the sixteenth century. Even then, there are considerable similarities between the two systems. Barring a few *Alamkaras*, the melodic patterns are interchangeable though the nomenclature is not always the same.

Contemporary Indian music can be divided into three major categories: I) Classical music, both of the North Indian and South Indian types; II) Folk music of the various regions and III) Popular music. Each of these are discussed below in relation to mass culture.

I. *Classical Music*

Although most of the discussion here will be restricted to North Indian classical music, some of the statements are equally applicable to South Indian classical music. Indian classical music today is full of new vigor. The development of North Indian classical music, both vocal and instrumental, has consisted of the elaboration by performers of the traditional *ragas*, which are considered fixed melodies. They are "traditional complex forms within which elaboration occurs. Considering its importance in Indian music, and how very seldom a new one becomes widely accepted, one might think of a *raga* as an unfinished masterpiece which is completed in an improvised performance."[12] "Improvisation," in Indian classical music, is not extemporaneous, but the result of long hours of practice for the creation of a single *alap* which can be described as rhapsodical embellishment[13] and a *tan* which is a rapid or slow rendering of the various combinations of the basic tunes of the *raga*.

The most common, prevalent, and well established form of vocal classical music today is the *Kheyal* or *Khyal*. This term means "imagination" and the form of music is so called because it is by nature imaginative both regarding subject-matter

12. Jerry Cohn, *An American Student and North Indian Music*, Delhi, 1965, p. 25.
13. W. Jones and N. A. Willard, *Music of India*, second edition, Calcutta, 1962, p. 29.

and interpretation. It is not bound by rigid rules except those pertaining to the use of the notes in the *raga*. The singing is usually divided into two parts. The first part is called *asthai*, in which the singer presents the words of the song and slowly develops the atmosphere characteristic to that *raga*, by gradually presenting the main body of the composition. The recurring metrical pattern or the *tal* is a slow rhythm. When the composition is fully developed and the proper atmosphere has been created, the singer presents the *antara* or the latter part of the song. This usually is sung in a faster tempo and and is full of *Cakri Tans*, which are rapid permutations of the specific notes of the *raga*.

In contemporary India there are five major schools of *Khyal* singing: 1) The Kirana School, best represented by Abdul Karim Khan. Its emphasis is more on the creation of the *Bhava* (emotion) and mood by a slow rhythmic presentation of a *raga*. The importance is to the tune and not so much to the word. 2) The Punjab School represented by Ustad Ghulam Ali; 3) The Gwalior School represented by Shankar Pandit; 4) The Jaipur School of Alladia Khan represented by Kesarbai Kerkar; and 5) The Agra School which incorporated much of the *Dhrupad* and *Holi-Dhamar* techniques. The best known singer of this school was Fayaz Khan.[14]

Since the classical period, most of the *ragas* have been associated with particular *bhava* and *rasa*. This has resulted in the association of certain combinations of tunes with heightened feelings of any one of the nine *rasas*. As a result, the emphasis has always been on creating an atmosphere which is conducive to certain emotions. However, outside of the most well-known *ragas*, there is no unanimity among scholars and singers as to which *ragas* create which feelings. In addition, many *ragas* are considered to create mixed emotions, just as the Sanskrit plays were expected to create the combination of various *bhavas* and *rasas;* the intention is to stimulate one emotion above the others.

Just as *ragas* are associated with certain emotions, some are also associated with particular seasons of the year, or with

---

14. Gosvami, op. cit., p. 131.

specific hours of the day. However, correlations of *ragas* with time and season have not remained constant, but have changed over a long period of time. The currently accepted conventions in this respect go back to the seventeenth and eighteenth centuries, and most professional singers still observe them. Another problem which arises concerning these restrictions is that whenever new combinations of two or three *ragas* are created — and this seems to be the new trend — quite often the component ragas of such combinations are sung at different times. These new "mixed" *ragas* are stretched over longer time periods and therefore there is more laxity in their presentations. Some of the famous morning *ragas* are: *Bhairav, Lalat, Todi-Asawari, Deskar*, in which there are a number of varieties. The afternoon *ragas* include *Sarang*, in which there are a number of variations, and for late afternoon *Bhimpalas, Multani, Poorvi* are sung. *Puriya, Suddha Kalyan, Bihag, Sankara, Bagesri, Kedara, Jaijaiwanti* are for the early evening while *Malkauns, Darbari Kanada, Basant*, and *Sohoni* are for the late evening.

Along with the *raga* composition, the other most important element of classical music is rhythm, which is indicated by *Tal*, meaning time-cycle. *Tal* consists of rhythmic time, measured in bars of a specific length, and composed of specific time-units, called *Matra*. There are about seven or eight most commonly used *Talas* which have different time-cycles with different time-units. The most popular is *Tin Tal* which consists of sixteen beats or time-units. When all the beats have been completed and the cycle starts again, the beginning point is called *Sam*. All the variations of the compositions performed have to be within the limitations of the *Tal;* generally the end of such a variation — called the *Tan* — must close at the *Sam*, or some other appropriate break (for example, in the middle of the cycle).

Although the classical music of India has retained its tradition over a long time and is often considered rigid, the history of its development clearly indicates that what are now recognized as established *ragas* were originally borrowed from folk tunes or tribal songs. The various names of the *ragas* suggest the different regions from which they originated, just as they also suggest their association with various seasons and states of nature. For example, the *raga "Pahadi"* means the mountain from where it was probably developed. *Raga "Basant"* represents the spring season, while *raga "Megha"* is associated with clouds and rain. There is no question that the classical music of today has assimilated a great deal of what was once an integral part of folk-music and has been formalized by following a specific structural model.

In the classical music of India today, especially in the *Kheyal* style of singing, there is almost no significance attached to the words. The greatest emphasis has always been on the tunes. As a result, the compositions have tended to become shorter and shorter, and quite often the singers are not even aware of the fact that the tunes and the emotive effect they create are inconsistent with the meanings of the words which go with the *raga*. The general practice is to sing the first part of the composition once and then to simply repeat the first phrase, since from then on, it is the combinations of the tunes alone which count.

On the whole, the nature of Indian classical music is such that there is no scope for individual innovation except in the presentation of the individual *ragas*.[15] Not very many musicians attempt to create new *ragas* and even if they do, only rarely does a *raga* gain such popularity that it is sung by other musicians. An important reason for the lack of such innovation is that it is often looked down on. During the nineteenth and early twentieth centuries, most of the famous Muslim and Hindu singers were not educated. They had no notions about innovations in classical music. The training they received was not systematic but was a direct imitation of their masters who in turn were extremely conservative and whimsical. The masters rarely satisfied the curiosity of the disciples by giving the *raga* names or their notations. The extreme pride of the individual schools prevented a disciple of one school from acquiring the style of other schools, or learning from notable singers of other schools. There was always a keen and open competition among the singers of these various schools. In this atmosphere a disciple was most acclaimed for

15. Cohn, op. cit., p. 30.

being able to imitate his *guru* to the best of his ability. Furthermore, the well-known singers were miserly in teaching their disciples everything they knew. There are literally hundreds of anecdotes about what even the most favorite pupil had to do to acquire the best available training from his *guru*. The teacher never allowed his disciples to write down the notations of the numerous *alaps* and *tanas*. It was only after Pandit Bhatkhande published his several volumes on classical music in the early twentieth century that some of the *raga* compositions became readily available.[16]

North Indian classical music by nature is such that it is most effective in a small gathering. Most of the notable singers until recently were under the patronage of the Maharajas and therefore sang only in the courts and palaces before select audiences. Public concerts were not popular until the later part of the nineteenth century.

Classical music, by definition, is structurally complex; one has to listen to it as frequently as possible over a long period of time before one begins to understand and appreciate it. The average Indian has neither the time nor the patience for this. In this respect, classical music is inaccessible to the masses. The same can be said about the musicians. Acquiring the necessary skill to perform classical music takes a long time, especially if it is to be learned in the traditional way. There is a belief that one has to practice for a period of twelve years before one can gain some mastery in Indian classical music. Therefore, one has to make performing classical music a lifelong devotion, and only a select few, either because of love or because of family tradition, can afford to invest this much time. Although the growing popularity of music schools and colleges indicates a trend away from the traditional way of learning classical music, there is still stigma attached to the expertise achieved through the professional schools instead of through a well-established maestro. A singer who expresses in his style a combination of various schools and is not identified as an exponent of a single school is still looked down upon by the "true" connoisseurs of music.

16. B. V. Keskar, *Indian Music: Problems and Prospects*, Bombay 1967, p. 37.

As the classical literature clearly indicates, at one time performing was considered to be exclusively the province of *ganika,* the sophisticated prostitute.[17] This attitude continued until recent times, so that performers automatically had a low status. Unless musicians became very famous, they were generally considered to be peculiar. This attitude, of course, is not restricted to India, but is generally true for the rest of the world. Society at large, while enjoying creative works, generally treats artists with some suspicion since they do not fit into the accepted patterns of behavior, and are not considered sociable.

During the last twenty-five years, however, the situation has changed. The growing emphasis on the arts, the emancipation of women, the extension of educational opportunity, and other modernizing trends have all helped to extend classical music to a larger audience, so that today it is considered "cultured" to know something about classical music, and "fashionable" to be an amateur performer. The popularity of the theater and the opera in the various regions has contributed to this development, since many famous songs in plays and in movies are based on the compositions of the well-known *ragas.* After independence, the Ministry of Broadcasting and Information under the leadership of B. V. Keskar systematically emphasized classical music by having weekly concerts broadcasted from the Delhi station of All India Radio. The Government of India every year honours musicians by offering them prizes and life pensions. In essence then, both the central and the state governments have taken over the role of patron, formerly one of the important functions of the Maharajas of the numerous princely states. Today many music festivals are held which last for three or four days and are attended by large audiences. The art of reviewing concerts in prominent newspapers and weeklies is also becoming popular. Long-playing records reached India during the last six or seven years, and now many old recordings of a single musician are put together on a single LP record. Famous artists like Ravi Shankar, Nikhil Bannerji, and Ali Akbar Khan have recorded their re-

---

17. Basham, op. cit., pp. 183-188.

citals, and these recordings have become popular both at home and abroad. Many young, promising artists such as Pandit Jasraj, Bhimsen Joshi, Nazakat and Salamat Ali, Kishori Amonkar have come out with recordings of their performances. These records get reviewed regularly in the English and the regional language newspapers. In Maharashtra, as in many other regions, many books on classical music are written for the consumption of educated, middle-class readers; these are anecdotal as well as analytical on the styles of musicians.[18] The growing interest shown by westerners in Indian classical music and the frequent foreign tours of the country's topmost performers have aroused popular interest still further. It is now fashionable for middle-class, educated women to be amateur singers, and young marriageable women claim that they know and sing classical music in order to increase their "value" on the marriage market.

Indian musicologists firmly believe that popularization lowers artistic standards and enables young artists to gain fame prematurely. They fear that as classical music becomes increasingly popular and artists perform for larger audiences, they will gradually succumb to the demands of the public which are often for singing in a semi-classical style — *Thumri, Kavali*, and occasionally even popular movie songs. This trend is most noticeable in the concerts performed for foreigners and university students. Some have expressed alarm that the "purity" of the various styles will disappear if no musicians follow them or pass them on to their disciples.

Much of the above is a reaction to change. Classical music in India is in transition and is reaching a stage similar to its counterpart in western cultures; the masses want to devour the arts which until recently were the exclusive domain of the elites. The earlier feudal structure in which the artist had to please only his patron, after which he was free to do as he pleased, has disappeared. Artists now have to depend on popular support for survival; it is natural for musicians to supply what the populace demands. Artistic performance has

---

18. The following are only two titles from among many books written in Marathi on Music. Gopalkrishna Bhobe, *Nad*, Bombay, 1966;. K. D. Dixit, *Sadaj-Gandhar*, Bombay, 1967.

thus become commercialized, as it does in all societies where there is an emerging mass culture. One of the most popular spectacles in today's concerts of classical music in India is what is popularly called *jugalbandi*. One can describe this best as a "fight" between the performer and the accompanying drum player.[19] For all practical and theoretical purposes, the drums are considered secondary to the vocal or instrumental artist, although the *tabla* player is expected to show his skill, usually when the other accompanying instruments in a vocal concert play while the singer is momentarily pausing. The drums are expected to be complementary to the performer, not in competition with him. Today, in many concerts, especially those for western audiences, there is often a *tabla* solo performance which is an opportunity for the drum player to show his skill. Many famous drum players have exaggerated notions about their achievements and their roles and are eager to show how they can confuse the performer by playing complicated pieces of rhythm. They often forget that the vocalist or instrumentalist has a triple role to play, namely, to give the appropriate emotive interpretation of the *raga* which is being sung, to stay within the limits of the composition while improvising, and at the same time remain bound by the time count of the rhythm pattern. On the other hand, the *tabla* player has only to concentrate on accompanying the soloist. The drum players often display their skill at the expense of the performer, so that the performer has to either go along, or resort to other gimmicks to control the drum player. The end result is that the proper emotive atmosphere of the *raga* is not created, because the artist is not allowed enough time to gradually develop the melody before he begins to perform the *tanas*. Still, the "fight" between the vocalist and the *tabla* player is a major attraction for a large number of concert-goers.

Another feature of such popular "fads" which are accepted by the instrumentalists is the group concert where two players together play a single *raga*. This can be interesting if they perform in such a way as to complement each other and thus present more variety in the *raga*. Often, however, the perfor-

---

19. Bhobe, op. cit., pp. 99-100 and Dixit, op. cit., pp. 58, 225.

mers try to outdo each other in demonstrating their individual competence and skill. If the two instruments are not of the same basic type, the result is unharmonious.[20]

The position of a classical musician can be determined on the basis of the following criteria: 1) Years spent in training; 2) evaluation by other professionals; 3) the status of the *guru* and the *gharana* "school" he represents; 4) devotion to the art; and 5) natural ability. These criteria are generally applied in the order given, and examples are often cited where an individual became a famous musician by years of hard work and excellent training although he did not have a good voice.[21] In the process of popularization of classical music, some of these criteria are dropped and new ones are added. For example, the general populace does not care how many years' training the individual has received, or how well he represents a particular school. As a result, the opinions of popular journalists are often substituted for the opinions of experts.

In sum then, it can be argued that the future of classical music in India today is bright, if one looks at its quantitative growth. Whether or not this will affect the high standards set by the earlier generations when classical music was exclusively the domain of the elites, remains to be seen.

II. *Folk Music*

Folk Music in India has long been an ignored province for the general masses, partly because folk culture was not given scholarly attention until after the British conquered India. During the British regime many foreign administrators collected material on popular songs in the various regions.[22]

Folk music in India is very closely associated with religion, although narrative and purely entertaining music is not un-

---

20. Dixit, op. cit., pp. 58-59.
21. G. Bhobe, *Sat Svarasri*, Bombay, pp. 24, 51, 82, and N. M. Kelkar, *Bhaskar Buva Bakhale*, Bombay, 1967, pp. 96-98.
22. One finds only British and other western names in the available bibliography of articles and books written in English on Indian folk music and folklore. See bibliography in H. Barua, *Folk Songs of India*, New Delhi, 1963.

common. In the Indian context the following types can be labelled folk music:

1. Songs of praise to the Gods, or the devotional songs. These are usually composed by well-known saints, such as Tulsidas and Mirabai in Northern India;[23] Tukaram and Namdeo in Maharashtra;[24] or Tyagaraja in the South.[25] However, there are others whose authorship is unknown. In each case, usually one God or reincarnation is praised or worshipped. For example, Tulsidas's devotional *dohas* are mostly praise of Rama, the most popular incarnation. In Maharashtra, Tukaram's *Abhanga* is in praise of *Vithal*, the deity of the *Varkari* sect, who is considered the incarnation of Visnu. The majority of people in these regions know at least some of these devotional songs and sing them either at home or in gatherings. In these songs the importance is on the words and not on the tunes.

2. Narrative songs based on mythology — the Mahabharata and the Ramayana. These are usually long and describe episodes from the lives of Krishna and Rama, the two most popular incarnations. Others deal with moral values. The narratives are sung by individuals, but all present join in to sing the refrains. Many wandering troupes, such as the *Yaksagana* in Mysore or the *Tamasha* performers in Maharashtra perform narratives.[26]

3. Special songs in each region which reflect social customs and are sung at particular ceremonies such as marriage, death, childbirth, naming, puberty, etc.[27] It is interesting that this type of singing is generally in the women's domain. They preserve these songs since they play a prominent role in these ceremonies.

4. Music which is sung at special religious festivals, which

---

23. Wm. Theodore de Bary, ed. *Sources of Indian Tradition*, New York, 1958, pp. 345 ff.
24. Ibid., p. 353.
25. T. V. Subba Rao, *Studies in Indian Music*, New York, 1962, pp. 151-190.
26. Balwant Gargi, *Folk Theatre in India*, Washington, 1966, pp. 73-88; 145-164.
27. M. M. Underhill, *The Hindu Religious Year*, London, 1921; and Oscar Lewis, *Village Life in Northern India*, New York, 1958, pp. 157-248.

again seem to be dominated by women. Such festivals are *Nagapanchami* (Serpent's Day), *Vata-Pournima* (Worship of the Banyan Tree), Birth of Krishna, *Narali-Pournima* (Coconut day), etc. [28] Most of these songs are praises of the respective deities in whose honor the day is celebrated. At other times they indicate the seasonal changes. Different regions, of course, emphasize different religious festivals, but some important ones such as *Diwali, Dasara,* or *Holi* (the Festival of Spring) are common in most.

5. Ballads or historical and narrative songs. These usually tell of famous battles in the more recent history of the region, or of other similar episodes, and are sung both for entertainment, group solidarity, and traditional pride. In Maharashtra, the *Pawadas* are such narrative songs; these describe the Peshwas and the battles the Marathas fought with the Moghuls and the British.[29] This has remained one of the most popular forms of mass entertainment. For example, in the agitation for a separate Maharashtra state, Amar Sheikh composed his own *Pawadas* and sang them all over Maharashtra. He became a very popular performer and thus helped gain momentum for the movement.[30] A similar type of ballad singing is the *Nautanki* performance in Uttar Pradesh, Punjab and Rajasthan.[31] Although formerly the *Pawada* was restricted to heroic events, it has been used for socio-political purposes in recent times and has, as a result, widened its scope of topics. During the Nationalist movement and the boycott of the Congress on the alcohol issue, there were many ballads composed on the ill-effects of drinking and the great advantages of abstinence. Thus, during the last two or three hundred years this type of folk music has had a powerful socio-political impact.

6. Love songs. These are essentially based on the life story of Krishna, especialy his early childhood, and his relationship with the milkmaids. The impact of the Bhakti movement in

---

28. Lewis, op. cit., pp. 197 ff.
29. Y. N. Kelkar, *Aitihasik Povade,* Poona, 1944.
30. S. Karhade, "Amarsekhanci Sokantika," in *Satyakatha,* October 1969, pp. 43-48.
31. Gargi, op. cit., pp. 37-49.

the fifteenth and sixteenth centuries over all of India made this type of devotion-cum-love composition the most popular form of folk-art; usually it was presented with dancing and acting. The *lavani* music in Maharashtra, and the *Jatra* performances in Orissa, Bengal, and Bihar use this type of singing.[32] Many other secular folk-theater performances use love songs as well, although the story may be based on a love episode of some famous historical hero, instead of the more popular *Ramlila* and *Raslila* which are based on love episodes in the life of Krishna and Rama. The listeners join in the chorus and also in chanting the names of the Gods.

The categories mentioned above are by no means clear-cut. Quite often a song may belong to more than one category; it may be devotional, and narrative at the same time. It may be a song reflecting social customs which are derived from certain religious observations. This is particularly common since many of the Hindu traditions and customs are deeply embedded in religion and it is difficult to separate the two. However, any music which falls into one of the above categories has distinct characteristics by which it is judged to be folk music. These are:

Simplicity of structure: Folk music is not so ornate and complex in its tonal structure as classical music. Neither is there an emphasis on the rigor of execution. Since most folk music is passed down from one generation to another in an informal manner, the overall compositional and tonal structure remains more or less the same. The individual singer is not aware of this; he simply sings the only way he knows.

Emphasis on word: In all folk music the text is very important, often more important than the music. If one knows the words well, one can sing them, no matter how poor the quality of one's voice. It is the words which evoke the emotions and establish the rapport between the singer and the listener. As a result, folk music relies heavily on oral tradition and is representative of the dialectical variation.

Emphasis on narration or storytelling: Most folk music is entertainment by way of storytelling. This is particularly true

---

32. Ibid., p. 18.

of the ballads. Simplicity of tonal structure helps the running narrative.

Group participation: Young and old, men and women, rich and poor, all join in singing, especially when the theme is a religious one, or if the singing is related to a particular festival. One of the reasons for this is the belief that by singing a devotional or religious song, one incurs merit. One of the basic tenets of Hindu philosophy is that the more often God's name is spoken, the higher the merit for the individual. In many cases the singer himself will encourage people to join in. This is often done in *Kirtan* where the *Kirtankar* — the performer — will sing a particular song appropriately related to the episode he is describing and at the end of the cycle will chant the name of the Lord Krisna or Rama and will ask the audience to join him. In various religious festivals, especially those where there is group worship of serpents, or the banyan tree, all women worship and sing together. Anyone who has been to a temple in any part of India will know that at the regular time of prayer, everybody present will join in and all the bells in the temple will be rung simultaneously. In Maharashtra, at the Pandharpur pilgrimage, the *Varkaris* (pilgrims) will gather on the bank of the *Chandrabhaga*, the river in the city of Pandharpur, and will sing *Bhajans*. There may be two or three hundred people standing in line with cymbals in their hands singing and dancing. This style has been adopted by the Hare Krishna movement in America.

Association with religious and social beliefs, superstitions, and social attitudes: The themes of many songs are often related to code of behavior towards members of the joint family; such relationships are often the topic of ridicule, humor, or moral advice. In this way, folk music reveals the behavior patterns of society.

On the whole, folk music seems much closer to mass culture because it is composed and performed by the nonelites; it's simple, straightforward, and narrative style is within the understanding of the masses who have neither the energy nor the motivation to understand the more complex classical music. The masses participate in folk music and enjoy it since it reflects their own hopes, disappointments, and lifestyles.

Folk music also reflects the considerable regional variety in India at the mass level. This diversity is overridden, however, by the simplicity, directness, and religious emphasis shared by all.

III. Popular Music

Film music in India must be considered as songs rather than themes. Judging by the tremendous popularity of the movie songs and the big revenue they bring in, it is safe to guess that no film is likely to be produced without songs in the near future. Compared with both classical and folk music, film music is a relatively new phenomenon, which began only in the 1930's, when the first talkies were produced.[33] One of the most well-known music directors of the Prabhat Film Company, Keshavrao Bhole, experimented first with film music.[34] Bhole did the very first musical films such as *Amrit Manthan* (*Churning of the Sea*), *Chandrasena*, *Kunku* (*The Mark of Marriage*), and *Sant Tukaram* (*The Saint Tukaram*). Bhole had imagination, and used various instruments, both Indian and western, to create the appropriate emotive effects. He never put songs into his films for their own sake, but always weighed the adequacy and proper timing. His background music was effective without being overbearing. As a result, all Marathi films and their Hindi versions produced by Prabhat became popular not only for the plots, direction and acting, but also for their excellent music. *Saint Tukaram* ran in Bombay for 57 weeks.[35] Bhole has described in detail how he contemplated each song, how often he rehearsed them, how he considered matching the aural and visual effects not only of the songs but also of the background music for each film.

By the end of the thirties, it was clear that film music had become the most popular form of mass entertainment. It was during and immediately after the war that film centers began to shift to big cities such as Bombay, Calcutta, and Madras. It was also apparent that Hindi movies would have the largest

---

33. E. Barnouw and S. Krishnaswamy, *Indian Film,* New York, 1963, pp. 83 ff and Panna Shah, *The Indian Film,* Bombay, 1950.

34. Keshavrao Bhole, *Majhe Sangit: Racana ani Digdarsan,* Bombay, 1964.

35. Barnouw, op. cit., p. 85.

commercial market, while films in regional languages would be restricted to their respective geographical areas. The great financiers and entrepreneurs began to see considerable profits in the film industry. As a result, more and more Hindi films began to be produced, even in non-Hindi areas. Madras became the biggest production center of Hindi films because of the availability of all facilities. The South Indian film companies entered the arena with their first spectacular, *Chandralekha*, which had everything, including war scenes, a circus, dances, and plenty of music.[36] The producers began to realize the importance of film songs since, even if the film were a failure, hit songs might result and thousands of records could be sold; copyrights for playing them on All India Radio and other commercial stations could earn them a considerable amount of money. Thus began the era of film music in which music was no more considered an integral part of the film, but an independent entity in itself.

By the early fifties, the ready-made formula for the success of any film was well established. Each film was to include a sentimental story in which both the hero and heroine go through all kinds of problems and finally unite. Each film was to include at least eight to ten songs and two or three dance sequences. It did not matter if these were relevant to the story or not. It was considered very prestigious to use as many instruments as possible, and it was not at all uncommon for a studio to have a staff of over fifty instrumentalists who played both the eastern and western instruments.[37]

The music director was to make at least two or three hit songs in whatever way possible. There was no question of observing tradition. Any mixture would do, so long as it caught the fancy of the public ear. As a result, film music became a strange mixture of Indian melody and western harmony. American jazz and Latin-American rhythms were regularly imitated but were often transformed beyond recognition.[38] A common scene in many theatres in cities like Bombay was that of the audience rhythmically keeping the beat of

36. Ibid., pp. 164-166, and Shah, op. cit., p. 110.
37. Barnouw, op. cit., p. 150.
38. Ibid., pp. 150-151.

the most popular song which was played even before the beginning of the show, or during the intermission. Street vendors and beggars thrived on copying popular film songs. This situation has continued over the years, and film music remains the most popular music of India today. Although the All India Radio, which is under the control of the Ministry of Broadcasting and Information, used to play film songs over its stations, this was discontinued in 1952, after B. V. Keskar became the Minister. This, of course, helped the commercial radio stations outside India, which play film music most of the time. Radio Ceylon is among the most popular radio stations in India. In recent years, however, All India Radio has started playing film music again.

As a result of the significant status accorded to songs and music in Indian films, singers in the film industry have become famous and have reached the stage where they can compete in status with actors and actresses. With the development of play-back singing, it is no longer necessary for an actor or actress to be a singer also. Until the forties, most actors and actresses were also singers. Now all they have to do is to move their lips in an appropriate manner while somebody else sings the songs for them.

In the keen competition of film singing, there is little in the way of training and hard work; most of the well-known singers are accidently "discovered." Once a singer is established as a favorite, he may sing all the male (or female) roles, whether or not a different kind of voice is called for. It seems that the Indian masses never get tired of hearing the same singer over and over in many movies. Among today's most well-known male film singers are Talat-Mahmud, Manna De, Mohamed Rafi, and Hemant Kumar. The most popular female songer is Lata Mangeshkar who is popularly known as Lata. She has by now performed playback music for over 100 films and has numerous records to her credit.[39] This emphasis on music in films has significantly affected the status of the music director, who is now considered just as important as the stars.

Needless to say, the critics and the elites have been aghast

---

39. **Shanta Shelke** et al., ed. *Lata,* Bombay, 1967. pp. 203-204.

over what the films present as music. The real connoisseurs rarely listen to film music, and claim that it can in no way qualify as art; it is a strange mixture of all styles and is devoid of any quality. Occasionally there are efforts to elevate film music by using classical raga compositions, but on the whole these attempts are not taken seriously.

The popularity of the film music can be attributed to the following factors: 1) Simplicity of composition: Usually the song has only one or two stanzas. The opening line is repeated many times, which helps the listener remember it. 2) Catching tunes: The directors go to extreme lengths to start the songs with a combination of tunes which will immediately catch the attention of the listener. 3) Quick tempo or rhythm: Most of the songs are sung with a quick tempo which again catches the attention of the listener. In this context, the Indian music directors have used western rhythms. Film music in India rarely makes an effort to borrow anything from folk music; a notable exception here is the *Apu* trilogy of Satyajit Ray.

This discussion of the three major types of music in India suggests that the relation of music to mass culture in India is not in any way different from that in other cultures. The only exception is film music, a direct legacy of westernization; it has become the most widespread form of musical expression transcending linguistic, social, and religious barriers. In this sense, popular film music is the more powerful unifying force in India, although ironically it stands for something which is not representative of her tradition.

7

TRADITIONAL FORMS OF MASS MEDIA IN MAHARASHTRA

K. Narain Kale

India is a vast country with a population of more than 500 truthful they may be to their vision and sincere with their million people with various religions, cults and traditions. During the last two centuries, the impact of Western civilization, as well as the British rule and growth of industrialization, have added some new dimensions to its static way of life and effected considerable transformations in its otherwise smooth and immutable course; but, on the whole, these modifications are merely slight adjustments to changing circumstances rather than a complete metamorphosis of its basic structure.

For this reason, India's neo-elites, who display their new visions and aspirations through modern art forms and new literature, cannot strike a sympathetic chord with the conservative spirit of the large masses of people, however honest and experience.

This does not mean that the Indian masses are by nature allergic to change, but that they prefer to move cautiously. They, too, can appreciate, digest, and absorb improvement and reform, but they have no patience with revolutionary rhetoric and do not like to be hurried, dragged, or jostled. Their preference is for traditional ideas and time-honored cultural media. This difference in temperament between modern individualistic artists and the common people has breached a wide chasm between them and caused a mutual feeling of alienation and distrust, to the point where they feel their mutual interests are not only at variance, but in opposition, to one another.

II

Such a clash of interests was, however, neither felt nor expressed when the modern British theater and (later on) the American motion pictures began to make inroads on the native media of folk culture. No genuinely conscious or intelligent protests appear to have been made, nor any kind of organized opposition against them launched, by either the exponents of the traditional media or the discriminating intelligentsia of those times.

This was so, firstly, because of the novelty and the dazzling glamour of the new media; and secondly, because they were considered to be a mere extension and improvement of what already existed in a cruder form, with, perhaps, some added splendor and technical improvements. The fact that the difference between them was not only of quantity but also of quality and that their forms and functions were not identical, but dissimilar, was totally lost sight of, and they were accepted for what they were worth with great enthusiasm.

Those who exploited these new arts were, however, under no illusion about them, and were fully conscious of their potential popularity. They had also no regard for, or concern with, the traditional media but knew how to make use of those traditional artistic elements which had the power to attract the masses.

Since the objective in exploiting the new arts was pecuniary, these elements were stressed with ample commercial shrewdness. They used words, color, forms, story interests, pious sentimentality, and love, as they were used in the older forms too, but with a new style and purpose. In the new plays and films, these elements were used to excite and amuse the audience; they had been the means of providing the masses with aesthetic joy, ethical values and creative standards.

The old media had their origins in religious traditions and were valued for their humanizing social influence. Their practitioners lived a life consecrated to the devotion of their deities, and their profession was a matter of faith and dedication to their ordained duties. In displaying their arts, they were not out to amuse and please, but to render service to their gods. Performances were not for financial gain, and those who enjoyed them made contributions as a sort of voluntary philanthropy. These media, therefore, had their roots in the authentic folk culture and were in fact the real social institutions.

The modern commercial entertainment media, on the other hand, borrowed all the superficial and flimsy elements of the old cultural media, becoming in effect, spurious imitators of the time-honored perennial models.

Thus it happened that the old media, lacking conscious and concerted efforts in their defense, soon began to lose their hold over the populace, and gradually succumbed. Ultimately they were reduced to the position of adjuncts of traditional public festivals and private religious family functions, and even there their significance was more symbolical than real.[1] Since they had their roots in religious observance, they did not become totally extinct; their forms and techniques are, somehow, still retained and cherished by their hereditary practitioners, as a matter of family pride and obligation, and passed on from generation to generation.

III

As Indian national consciousness grew, political activists sought an effective popular means of awakening the interest of the masses. They turned their attention to this new arttheater, which they turned into a powerful propaganda instrument. Seemingly mythological and historical themes were infused with subtle, political allusions designed to create feelings of distrust and hatred for British rule and British bureaucracy, and feelings of contempt for Indians who collaborated with them. Maharashtra paved the way in this, and the other provinces followed suit.[2]

Any hope of completely transforming the traditional mass media in this direction was apocalyptic, although politicization was occasionally utilized by Tilak and his followers in the national birthday celebration of the festivals of historical heroes like Shivaji, Rana Pratap and others.

1. A. J. Agarkar, *Folk Dances of Maharashtra*, Bombay, 1950, pp. 26-44.
2. Vasant S. Desai, *The Marathi Theatre*, Bombay: Popular Prakashan, 1961, p. 26.

The evolution of Indian mass media has occurred in the context of Indian culture, and is rooted in a long history which varies as to language, habitat, climate, customs, superstitions, and faith. Underneath it all is the solid rock-base of an intense involvement in religion and human endeavour. It is natural that different parts of India should have different mass media, and yet at the same time possess a basic character that is the same. I would here concentrate on Maharashtra and its mass media to illustrate the forms and functions of mass media.

IV

Puppet shows, *Gondhala*, *Bharuda*, *Dashavatara* and *Lalita* are the principal cultural mass forms of Maharashtra. Most of them had become almost extinct by the beginning of this century, but since independence in 1948 strenuous efforts, both by the government and the people of Maharashtra have been made to revive most of them.

(1) *Puppet shows*: The work *Saikheda*, meaning a puppet show, has been used, and the performance mentioned, by Dnyaneshwar in his famous commentary on *Bhagwad-Geeta*, written in A.D. 1280. There is no doubt that these shows were current and popular in Maharashtra, then and after. They do not seem to have been indigenous to this region, but occasionally presented here by their exhibitors from Andhra, Karnatak, Rajasthan and other parts of India.

(2) *Keertana*: *Keertana* is one of the oldest of Indian mass media and the ancient sage Narad is believed to be its founder and foremost exponent.

This form is current in Maharashtra in two styles. In the first, which is most in vogue amongst the *Varkaris*, or the pilgrim devotees of Dnyaneshwar Tukaram sect, the performer of the *Keertana* selects a popular didactic text usually from the compositions of Dnyaneshwar or Tukaram, for his sermon and goes on expounding and amplifying its contents, explaining their esoteric meaning and significance. The continuous flow of this discourse is every now and then interspersed with prayers or *Bhajans*, chanted in unison by the entire crowd of the listeners along with the performer, and an atmosphere of abundant ecstasy and piety is made to prevail throughout the course of the performance. It is claimed that Vishnu had himself promised Narada that he would be personally present wherever his devotees sing his praise in such a *Keertana*.[3]

The second style of the *Keertana* form is better organized, more sophisticated, and more elaborately worked out as an artistic performance. It provides ample opportunities for the dramatic rendering of its subject matter, with a beginning, a middle and an end.

In this style the performer begins his sermon by singing the text of a suitable theme song and goes on elucidating its purport with pertinent explanations and comments, making his own critical observations and providing ample choice quotations from literature and scriptures. This brings the first part of his sermon to a close, as he reverts again to the theme song from where he originally started.

In the second part he again resumes the thread of his theme song and begins the narration of some story or episode, illustrating its moral. This provides him with plenty of opportunities to introduce any number of references to topics of contemporary interest in the course of his sermon, without being accused of any sacrilege or blasphemy; and to interlace his eloquence with rhetoric, dramatic irony, satire, parody and mime. He can almost make a one-man show of it. The *Sangeet Natak* (operetta) of Maharashtra, in fact can be said to have originated from this style of *Keertana*,[4] and the Sangeet theater to have influenced its later development. It was *Keertana* which the politicians of the Tilak school exploited so successfully for propaganda purposes.[5]

(3) *Gondhal*: Goddess Amba or Bhawani is the ancestral deity of many Maharashtrian families of all castes. The worshippers of Bhawani (so designated by heredity) are called *Bhutyas* or *Gondhalis*; giving song recitals in her praise and performing "sermons" or *Gondhals* describing her acts of prowess is their ordained profession. The recitals of *Gondhal*

---

3. Mahadeo Shastri Joshi, (ed.) *Bharatiya Sanskriti Kos*, Poona, 1964, Vol. II, pp. 350-52.
4. Desai, op. cit., p. 12.
5. Joshi, op. cit., p. 351.

are given in the *jatra* festivals of Bhawani, celebrated during the first nine days of the month of Ashwina of the Hindu calendar, or under certain circumstances, at the request of private individuals. Some of the *Gondhalis* are adept at composing ballads or lays of historical heroes, mythological gods, and persons celebrated for their good deeds, and singing them to village crowds, with suitable gestures.

Several Brahamin families in Maharashtra observe as a *kulachar*, or family custom, the practice of inviting a *Gondhali* minstrel to perform his *Gondhal* in honor of Bhawani whenever there is a wedding, a childbirth, or a house warming; although such performances are sponsored by individual families, they are considered to be public functions, and the entire community of the village is entitled to attend them.

During the years 1892-1906, a period of political agitation in Maharashtra, there was a serious attempt to revive this tradition of minstrelsy. The Savarkar brothers and Govind Darekar were its leading nonprofessional exponents.

(4) *Bharud*: This medium seems to have a close kinship with the *Bharads* of Gujarat and is very popular with the *Varkari* sect in Maharashtra. Eknath has written several compositions for *Bharud* and they give a colorful picture of the secular life of his times. They contain allegorical descriptions of the administrative affairs of the state, accounts of professional dealings, and amusing descriptions of sundry human types. Some of them are in the style of formal petitions or reports, while the others are in the form of narrative or lyrical songs. They are mostly metaphorical and deal with matters of everyday life in the context of the order of divine dispensation.

Bharuds are performed in private or community religious festivals and celebrations; and song, dance and mime seem to be their main features. The profession is hereditary, descending in families from generation to generation and its practitioners are supposed to maintain themselves on public philanthropy.

(5) *Dashavatar*: *Dashavatar*[7] is the dramatic representation

6. Ibid., Vol. III, p. 121.
7. Bapurao Naik, *The Marathi Theatre,* Bombay: Popular Prakashan, 1961.

of the story of the ten incarnations of Vishnu. It used to be staged by the inhabitants of the villages themselves in the festivals of local deities, with peasants, agricultural laborers, and artisans generally the main participants.

Of the ten incarnations, the episodes of Vaman, Ram and Krishna are usually played at great length, with elaboration and minute details; that of Narasinha is most often conveyed only in a sketchy suggestion. This is done as a precaution, since several actors in that role are said to have been so overpowered by the frenzied passion of Narasinha, that they have actually torn open the belly of Hiranya Kashyapu, the demon king, with their steel claws. The representation of Buddha and Kalki is usually omitted for lack of any legends about them.

The eternal clashes and conflicts between the gods and the demons is the theme of the *Dashavatars*, and armed fights and physical violence are not therefore tabooed in their performance. Anachronisms and absurdities are allowed a free rein; and a fictitious character called *Shankasur*, clad in the motley clothes of a circus clown, is introduced during the performance. This character correlates current events with the mythological incidents and personages; he appears to be an imitation of the devil of the Christian moralities, since *Dashavatar* was one the most popular cultural forms in Goa and is known there under the name *Dahikala* or merely *Kala*.[8]

(6) *Lalita*: The festivals of local deities were generally concluded with a *Lalita*, "the happy end." This is a kind of variety show in which anyone from the village community could volunteer to participate. It was a sort of "free for all" program and was looked upon as great fun. The unity of the show was maintained by the employment of a character called *Balsantosh* or "Child delight." The person playing this role had to have a buoyant sense of humor and a quick, ready wit. His role was to put an end to all bickerings and arguments in the program, level casual but pertinent criticism and comment on certain chosen members of the community for their particular deeds or words, and maintain, throughout, the jolly and

---

8. Agarkar, op. cit., p. 38.

carefree atmosphere. He was to conclude each witty observation and remark with the refrain, "Baba, bal Santosh" ("Father, the child is happy"), meaning "Good, bad or indifferent, everything is a part of the game, dear!" And all this he had to do extempore.

(7) *Tamasha*[9]: *Tamasha* seems to have been in vogue under that name for about a couple of hundred years, and the last Peshwa, Bajirao II, was one of its ardent admirers and celebrated patron. In his book *Folk Theatre of India*, Balwant Gargi, the author, has characterized this form as the most crystallized folk theater form in Maharashtra and described it at great length.[10]

Tamasha, however, has its roots in a secular tradition. It is not associated with any cult of worship and has little purposive social context.

Tamasha is a commercial entertainment form which originated in the camps of the mercenary soldiers of the Mohammedan invaders of India, and later on was performed in the armies of the Mahrattas. Its recent popularity derives from the predilection of theater proprietors to rent their theaters to *Tamasha* troupes at cheap rates on days and at times when no regular plays are billed there. This of course is not an act of charity, since they regard *Tamasha* as the lucrative supplementary wing of the legitimate commercial theater.

The artistes in *Tamasha* are the slaves of 'their patrons' whims, and the *Tamasha* singer has to sing for cash payment the songs of their patrons' preference, as they call out *Doulat-Ziada*— "May the wealth of the donor increase!" All the *Tamasha* troupes are private enterprises, and the star value of the female artiste is the troupe's main draw. This is in direct contrast to the accepted aesthetic standards for Indian cultural mass media.

V

The people of Maharashtra are theatrical enthusiasts, and

9. Joshi, op. cit., Vol. IV, pp. 39-43.
10. Balwant Gargi, *Folk Theatre of India*, Seattle: The University of Washington Press, 1966, pp. 73-88.

their new acquaintance with the Victorian theater fired their imagination with a new fervor. Dozens of professional companies of actors came into existence and began touring the region from one end to another. Private clubs for amateur productions were formed by educated and well-to-do theater enthusiasts in cities and towns, and theater became one of the most important adjuncts of their life.

In the wake of such a widespread craze it was natural for religious public festivals to succumb to the theatrical influence; the new literates who had begun to consider their traditional *Dashavataras*, *Bharudas*, and *Lalitas* stale and outdated were eager to welcome innovation. It arrived in the form of staging plays in a new style which imitated the city amateur productions. There was no dearth of talent or enthusiasm anywhere, and the festivals provided justifiable occasions for groups of local young men to stage a new style play which soon was readily accepted as a routine part of the celebrations. In the course of time such performances becames their regular and permanent features, and thus a new medium was added to the existing old ones, which were fast losing their general attraction.

In the western part of Maharashtra, especially in the Konkan districts of Ratnagiri and Kolaba, there are several villages which proudly claim that the custom of staging plays at village festivals has survived uninterrupted for more than a hundred years. In large towns, where there are several temples instead of one, more than half a dozen such festival performances are enacted every year, and they are packed not only by local crowds but by a large number of visitors from the surrounding villages and towns. Young village men who reside for months in the cities for employment or business, every year make it a point to return to their native places for the festivals which are special occasions in which they enthusiastically take part.

These performances are free of any charge and admission is open to all the members of the community without any distinction of caste or creed, without any privileges or priorities. The spectators sit on the ground, sometimes on their own mats. Costumes and stage props, are hired from the professional dealers in theatrical property if the play chosen is a costume drama; but if the play happens to be a social one, such necessities are either provided by the actors themselves or borrowed from the local gentry. The festival play performance is generally the most popular item of the celebrations, and is the talk of the place, for days and years to come.

VI

The definition of "mass" is now variable, depending on the user and the context. The stability and progress of a developing country rests on how "mass" opinion is formed and how "mass"-action is directed and consolidated. In a vast, kaleidoscopic, rural country like India, the mass media play a crucial role in shaping the future of the nation; and consequently, the consideration of their forms and functions is of utmost importance.

Conditions of life in India are now enormously changed from what they were, not only since 1920 but since 1948. Illiteracy is fast disappearing; books, periodicals, radio, and films are widening horizons of culture; faster and powerful means of communication are cutting out distances and bringing the people of the whole world closer together. The culture which once was the privilege of a chosen few at the center is now spreading over the area of the whole circle.

As in former times, India is challenged with the task of utilizing new forms of mass media in ways which will benefit society as a whole rather than the mercenary interests of a few. The existence as well as the magnitude of this challenge is not something of which the present generation is unaware. Attempts to meet it have already been made on various levels and with diverse approaches. The one point common to all of them is the importance of the old media and the significance of their study for future guidance. What is needed above all, however, is some positive course of action.

Those involved in the problem know that the old mass media have characteristics which have given them their lasting power and popularity. Most of them have a religious base; their performances have a social objective; their performers are not responsible to any individual or authority, but are devoted to a cause; and the relationship between them and the recipients of their arts is free from any consideration of sale and purchase or patronage and dependence.

They also know that the revival of the old mass media, in their original form, is totally out of the question because their inevitable religious bias is no longer tenable in the new age. The only course to follow, therefore, is to infuse them with a new spirit by introducing certain modifications in their forms, that is, to reform them to suit the requirements and demands of the modern times. They believe that based on past precedents, reformism will not antagonize the masses but that it will be acceptable to them as a matter of course. Tilak did that with *Keertana;* his followers did it in the case of the theater; and Satyashodhak Samaj tried a similar experiment with *Tamasha.* The same example will have to be followed and emulated even now, whether in attempting to adapt the old media to new forms or devising new media for future use.

The temples of various gods and goddesses have so far served as the citadels for the old mass media, but whether they should be expected to be used as such in future, with their religious basis eliminated is debatable. As a matter of practical experience, however, it is a well-known fact that several religious temple festivals have already begun to include in their program a large number of secular items that have no relationship whatever to their religious character. The practice of performing stage plays is an example.

This change in the organization of religious temple festivals has a vital and close bearing on the question of devising new mass media; consequently, it needs careful consideration. Only last year, I myself had the rare opportunity of attending such a modernized religious temple festival in a village called Padghavali, in Kolaba district. What I observed there was extremely enlightening.

The occasion was the annual birthday celebration festival of the god *Ganesha,* on the fourth day of the month of Magha of the Hindu calendar; and all the inevitably necessary religious and ritualistic ceremonies were rigidly observed and performed as a matter of course. But the main emphasis of the celebration was the social and artistic items of the program, and they were, in fact, the ones which were most enthusiastically anticipated, ably performed and largely attended. The traditional media such as *Keertan*, *Bharud* and *Lalita* had their own places, but the performance of a modern stage play and the recital of the *Geeta-Ramayana* composed by Gajanan Madgulkar, were the items which were most eagerly awaited, and cheerfully received and acclaimed when presented.

Most of the inhabitants of the place who otherwise reside in cities like Bombay or Poona for employment or business had returned home to spend the occasion with their families; people from the nearby localities had also flocked there as guests of the local gentry. Amongst those present were solicitors, doctors, auditors, accountants, advocates, principals and professors of colleges, editors and columnists of newspapers and periodicals, merchant industrialists, jewelers, teachers, clerks and well-to-do gentlemen of various occupations. But all these members of the so-called higher classes were mixing freely and participating enthusiastically in the functions of the festival without the least indication of any sense of superiority or exclusiveness, with groups of the masses composed of peasants, domestic servants, farm laborers, artisans, and men and women of the aboriginal Katkari tribe.

Not men alone, but women, too, had their share in the program of the festival, almost in equal proportion. Besides the routine program, some programs with educative and social intent were organized for women only, and highly educated, well-dressed society ladies from rich families were seen rubbing shoulders with illiterate and ill-clad women of the working classes, without any consciousness of superiority, class distinction, or loss of dignity.

The temple, of which this festival is an accessory function, is in fact the temple of a family deity and private property. But conditions are so much changed now by customary practice that the festival is now looked upon and treated as a public institution and is organized and managed in an institutional manner.

This festival at Padghavali is not a solitary or an exceptional example of such religious temple-festivals in Maharashtra; but at the same time it must be remembered that its Catholic and comprehensive form and its institutionalization has not been achieved by chance or coincidence but by deliberate and conscious planning and organization. It is only through such experiments and efforts that the dream of evolving new mass media and providing suitable citadels for their display will ever come true.

8

THE INFLUENCE OF MASS CULTURE ON FOLK CULTURE IN A MYSORE VILLAGE

Helen Ullrich

As a phenomenon of an advancing technology, mass culture is spreading throughout India. Although mass culture has not yet permeated all forms of literature and art, folk culture has already been strongly influenced. It is the purpose of this paper to examine changes in folk literature and art which have occurred in this period of advancing technology in India.

Art forms reflect the technology of the era in which they are produced. An advanced technology enables the mass production of art, as well as of consumer goods. Not only does the average man have an opportunity to raise his standard of living, but he may also have the leisure to enjoy literature and art. A market demand will lead to a production of literature and art for mass consumption. Literature and art produced for mass consumption may be considered mass culture.

Before the development of mass production and mass media, there were two kinds of art and literature — high art and folk art. High art was the domain of the elite who had the necessary wealth to commission artists, poets, and musicians and the necessary education to appreciate the products of their patronage. In a basically illiterate society the elite were the literati. High art in India was linked to the "Great Tradition." As a spontaneous development of the people themselves, folk art and literature were primarily local phenomena.

Mass culture, high art, and folk art all have their own characteristics. The predominant characteristics of genuine mass culture are standardization, stereotypy, and conservatism.[1] High art, in contrast, is esoteric, personal, and individualistic. Folk art, like mass culture, is exoteric. Unlike mass culture which is mass produced for an uninstructed, unrestricted public, folk art arises from and consequently is an expression of the people themselves.

Bernard Rosenberg has postulated that "modern technology is the necessary and sufficient cause of mass culture."[2] Modern technology is not generally associated with a peasant society such as India. The development of an advanced technology in what was essentially a peasant society is a result of Westernization. The British entry into India opened channels for education which were eagerly utilized despite caste prohibitions. Among foreign educated Indians there arose an awareness of and motivation for a more advanced technology. Western contact, in fact, provided India with the means to develop the technology requisite for mass culture. Insofar as the development of technology in India is a consequence of Westernization and not of internal modernization, mass culture in India is a product of Westernization.

Just how extensively Indian mass culture is an emulation of western mass culture is difficult to measure. Among the high castes Westernization provides a means for maintaining distance from the Sanskritizing lower castes. The western mass culture which is currently sought after by the high caste, westernized group may become part of Indian mass culture when the Sanskritizing castes realize its status value. Teenagers who are attending private schools manifest great interest in western popular music. If this aspect of Westernization becomes available to teenagers in general, western popular music may become part of Indian mass culture. Now, those who value western popular music are limited to a small, highly westernized high caste group. The teenager who does not have access to western popular music, such as those of

---

1. Leo Lowenthal, "Historical Properties of Popular Culture," *Mass Culture: The Popular Arts in America*, edited by Bernard Rosenberg and David Manning White, Glencoe, Illinois: The Free Press, 1957, p. 55.
2. Bernard Rosenberg, "Mass Culture in America," in Rosenberg *et al.* op. cit., p. 11.

Totagadde,[3] has no interest or knowledge in western popular music. But the opinion expressed in Totagadde that those from the areas where teenagers value western popular music are a half century ahead suggests a situation favourable for emulation. Whether such emulation will be confined to small groups or will become part of the widespread Westernization-Sanskritization dichotomy remains to be seen. That Indian mass culture has developed along its own lines is clear from calendar art and films.

Films and calendar art are the most obvious forms of mass culture in the village of Totagadde.[3] These coexist with folk literature such as folk drama, tales, music. In Totagadde there is a sharp schism between the literature and art the elders appreciate and the youth appreciate. The value placed on mass culture corresponds inversely to the value placed on folk culture. Only rarely does a young person know folk tales and *harikatha;* these are the speciality of old women. With the exception of calendar art, the elders do not appreciate mass culture. In general, their interests revolve around traditional religious culture. When the youth put on a social drama in the village, the elders express the opinion that episodes from the epics are more entertaining and suitable for dramatization. Unlike the elders, the youth have not learned oral literature, but prefer to read, attend movies, or listen to the radio.

The change from an illiterate society to a literate society and the introduction of mass culture occurred almost simultaneously. The older people rarely had an opportunity to attend school. Those who did attend school, some of the Brahmin men, went to the *pathshala,* a Sanskritic school, where they learned to read Sanskrit and to recite the Vedas. The oral tradition and traveling troupes provided the main sources for entertainment. The elders have retained their appreciation for folk art and literature. The youth, in contrast, are all literate. At first, some of them had to fight for the right to attend school — even to the extent of running away

3. Totagadde, a pseudonym, is a village approximately two hundred miles northwest of Bangalore. Fieldwork in Totagadde was conducted during the years 1964-66 under the auspices of the American Institute of Indian Studies.

to school. Perhaps as a result of the effort which was exerted to obtain education, it has become a highly valued commodity. At present, the more educated a woman is the better marriage her father can arrange for her. Educational facilities have evolved so that one can even live at home and attend college. Everyone in the village is expected to attend grammar school. Havik Brahmin girls are expected to complete high school and may go on to college. Men are expected to go through college. Academic failure rather than financial or personal difficulties has become the primary reason for dropping out. With the increase in education has come a diversification of interests. Reading and attending movies are popular pastimes with the youth.

Accompanying the increase in education has been a decrease in concern about ritual pollution. Generally a girl will stay at home for the period when she is in a state of ritual pollution. However, if she is away from the village, she ignores the ritual pollution associated with menstruation. When she is at home, she may now read and study anything except the scriptures. The offense to the goddess of learning, Saraswati, is ignored. The older women would not have been allowed to read. But now the days of ritual pollution are spent reading. It is not surprising that women do more reading than men.

The decrease in observing ritual pollution has increased mobility. Only a few bother to wash off the pollution acquired in the city when they return home. Travel to and from town has been facilitated by this revision of pollution rules. This lack of concern with ritual pollution gives the younger people more freedom to enjoy forms of mass culture in town such as movies and drama than older people who worry about being polluted. Seating arrangements at the movies and plays are not along caste lines.

The dance drama, *Yakshagana*, provided a thread of continuity between mass culture, folk culture, and high culture. Traceable to the days of *Vijayanagara*, *Yakshagana* was and still is performed at religious centers and by traveling troupes associated with temples. The apprenticeship period required to learn *Yakshagana* properly is a minimum of five years for actors and *maddale* (drum) players, and two years for *chande* players. From the beginning, apprentices, who may be as young as eight years of age, are trained both on the stage and with a teacher. In the fifth year the apprentices play young characters such as Arjuna's son Abhimanyu and Karna's son Vrishisena, Arjuna's brothers, Sahadeva and Nakula. They will then dance these roles until they are about thirty or until they gain role priority by being among the older members of the troupe. While gaining stage experience, apprentices learn either to dance and talk or play the drums. As prescribed by high culture, *Yakshagana* requires a long apprenticeship and has a handbook *Subhalaxana*.[4] But all is not prescribed. The dialogue and acting are learned through observation. Reliance on improvization is a characteristic of folk art. The lack of dialogue codification enables the actors to develop their own skills at repartee and to apply the epic to the present day. The adaptation of the epics to the modern day has perhaps bastardized *Yakshagana* as high culture. At the same time it has caught the imagination of many. The post-harvest arrival of the *Yakshagana* traveling troupes is eagerly awaited by the folk in Totagadde. People of all ages look forward to the arrival of the traveling troupes from South Kanara. The troupes are generally associated with temples and perform at temples as well as go on tour after the harvest.

Before the advent of mass culture in India, the "Great Tradition" of the contemplative few emanating from the great religious centers, temples, monasteries and pilgrimage places provided an umbrella of commonality over the diversity of the "Little Tradition." From these centers, religious mendicants, actors, *Yakshagana* troupes, and singers all went forth carrying a common traditional culture to the hinterland. The great temples, monasteries, and pilgrimage places provided both a meeting place for people from diverse regions to sally forth with the "Great Tradition" tales for the people back home and acted as a relay station from which it sent its own emissaries forth. *Yakshagana,* as one type of emissary from these centers, spread aspects of the "Great Tradition" to the masses at that time. Even today annually the first and last performances of

4. Information was provided by Martha Bush Ashton in correspondence.

all the troupes are given in front of the temple of their affiliation. Episodes from the *Mahabharata*, the *Ramayana* and the *Bhagavatha Purana* provide the material for the *Yakshagana* drama. One might conceive of these as representatives of the traditional religious culture of this period. The "Great Tradition", bearing the religious culture now contrasts sharply with the multi-faceted aspects of modern mass culture which nevertheless includes adaptations from the "Great Tradition's" religious culture.

The carriers of modern mass culture are also more diverse than the carriers of the "Great Tradition". Traveling troupes still come, but the importance of these has been replaced by the radio, movies, novels, newspapers, and magazines. The radio which generally occupies a prominent position on the front porch, provides background noise as well as news, music, social-drama, traditional drama, and *Yakshagana*. The most popular movies follow the formula of a melodrama with a happy ending and much singing and dancing. Novels are read primarily by women, who like sentimental novels, psychological novels, and comedies. Both traditional classical drama and social criticism have been performed in the village. The youth prefer social criticism; the elders, religious drama based on the epics.

This preference of the youth in Totagadde may be deduced from the fact that they no longer study *Yakshagana* as a hobby.[5] Although the *Yakshagana* traveling troupes were associated with temples, *Yakshagana* performances were not limited to these professional troups. Men of a village or surrounding villages frequently got together and performed *Yakshagana*. The term *Yakshagana*, literally *yaksha* "demi-god," and *gana* "song," (e.g., "songs of the demi-god") refers to the dance drama itself. Elaborate costuming and make-up stereotype the characters. The kings, warrior heroes, and romantic heroes are known by their oval, fluted, or pointed crowns. Vishnu and his incarnations, primarily Rama and Krishna, wear the *kireeta* crown, which is "surmounted by a lotus, flanked by

---

5. In South Kanara, *Yakshagana* is popular among students who perform at school functions. Personal communication with Peter Claus and Martha Bush Ashton.

two graceful swans with red flowers in their beaks, the whole being topped with peacock feathers. Filmy red or white drapery flows from the back of the crown and is tucked in the waistcoat at either side".[6] Romantic characters such as the Gandharvas wear pear-shaped head-dresses. Demons and "terrifying aspects of divinity" such as Narasimha have individualized make-up. The remaining characters wear dress appropriate to their roles. Such elaborate costuming accompanies the drama whenever the dancing is performed. *Yakshagana* enthusiasts sometimes gather to sing and play the music. This is known as *tala maddala*. *Tala Maddala*, the *Yakshagana* without dancing and costumes, is generally performed during the monsoon, when an outdoors performance with costumes and dancing would be impossible. Few of the Totagadde men who performed *tala maddala* are still alive. It would appear that the popularity of *Yakshagana* is decreasing.

It indeed appeared that *Yakshagana* in its old form was a dying art when Shivram Karanth, a Puttur patron, attempted to save *Yakshagana* from extinction by popularizing it. His efforts have resulted in saving the dance-drama, but not in its widespread popularity. There are now twelve professional troupes associated with temples, but no longer are there family troupes. Fewer traveling troupes come to Totagadde but they play and dance to much larger audiences than before. Modern technology has provided technical assistance such as microphones, so that a large audience can be accommodated.[7] A more business-like management has also resulted in charging for performances.

Although the rules and regulations involving ritual purity are generally not followed as closely now as before, at *Yakshagana* performances the seating arrangement according to caste is as strictly followed as ever.[8] More people can and do

---

6. Martha Bush Ashton, "Yakshagana: A South Indian Folk Theatre," *The Drama Review*, Spring 1969, p. 150.

7. Information about the most recent developments in Totagadde have been conveyed by Edward B. Harper.

8. Martha Bush Ashton and Peter Claus both report that seating arrangements at *Yakshagana* performances in South Kanara are not according to caste.

attend each *Yakshagana* performance. At the same time that each caste member is being more strongly reminded of his place at the village *Yakshagana* performances, *Yakshagana* has been democratized by radio performances. The ritualization, on the one hand, and democratization, on the other, is not without parallel. A less than ritualistic village priest was deposed and replaced by the most orthodox man in Totagadde. When the temple was reconsecrated, a *Yakshagana* troupe was specially commissioned to perform. This use of the troupe to carry "Great Tradition" religious messages to the village may be somewhat analogous to earlier roles of such troupes. In the seventh, eighth, and ninth centuries A.D., the religious faith of the people was threatened constantly by the uncertain political conditions in the country. The Brahmins took it upon themselves to spread their religion and preserve the dance-drama, using each for the benefit of the other.[9]

The case of *Yakshagana* illustrates an art form in transition from folk culture to mass culture. The advance in technology in India and the advent of the radio and the microphone make possible the production of art forms for the masses. Yet the role *Yakshagana* plays in various areas of Mysore differs so radically that I cannot pretend to speak about more than one. In this area, mass culture may range from the latest film music to the most classical of *ragas*.

---

9. Ashton, op. cit., p. 153.

9

MEDIEVAL BENGALI CULTURE: THE NONELITE ELEMENTS

TAPAN RAYCHAUDHURI

In a transitional society with a background of classical civilization, the elements of continuity in the culture of all those whose modernization is as yet incomplete are likely to be very marked. This paper attempts to explore the affinities and continuities of the contemporary nonelite to its counterpart in the premodern culture. Bengal was deliberately chosen as the area for study. It was one of the regions where the balance of power between the Hindu "Great Tradition" and local "Little Tradition" was, if anything, tilted in favour of the latter. The distinct articulation of a local culture emphasized this fact and the relevant developments took place during the period of Turko-Afghan and Mughal rule known as the medieval period, in popular parlance. Medieval Bengali culture, with its strong nonelite bias (the local elite culture was closely linked to the "Great Tradition") is in some ways a counterpart of modern mass culture. It is not suggested, however, that they are similar.

The term "culture" raises some conceptual problems. For the anthropologist, the term includes all artifacts, material or otherwise, used and transmitted by society. This is far more comprehensive a meaning than the popular use, which refers mainly to intellectual and artistic activities and the ideas and feelings associated with them. The popular concept is, however, wider than is apparent at first sight; "culture" refers not merely to the books one reads or the music one hears, but the furniture one uses and the food one eats — in short, to the entire lifestyle. The term "mass culture", though not clearly defined anywhere, is closer in meaning to the popular than the anthropologist's usage. Studies of mass culture tend to be widely inclusive although the limits are not precisely drawn. The term "culture" is used in this paper in the same imprecise sense.

Contemporary mass culture has some distinctive features which are necessarily absent in earlier phases of technology. Its main properties are the media of mass communication, heavily dependent on modern technology, and almost equally modern specialized organizations. Hence, in terms of scale — the sheer size of the mass audience and the degree of cultural homogeneity or uniformity that can be generated — it has no precedents in history. Its main roots are in contemporary life which is marked by features of sharp discontinuity with the past, owing to a vastly changed environment. The element of transmission, of inheritance from the past, is minimal in mass culture, though it is in the process of creating its own myths, archetypes and values which may be transmitted to the future.

There are, however, essential affinities between modern mass culture and mass culture in the earlier phases of history. In all complex civilizations, a high culture and a low culture have been present. The latter demands a relatively low level of cultivation or training for its comprehension and enjoyment; this is true of even the creative effort, though there might be important exceptions to it. Ease of communication is another common base of popular culture, both modern and premodern. It is dependent on familiarity with a particular cultural idiom which, even though complex, is imbibed in the course of one's social existence and not learnt through strenuous effort. Modern mass media imparts the necessary familiarity to a very wide audience. The relatively parochial character of popular cultures in earlier ages derived partly from the limitations of the media of communication, though classical civilizations devised instruments of transmission and propagation which were remarkably effective over time.

The historic culture of the rural peasant community is explained by the concept of the "Little Tradition". As a descriptive label for the culture of the common people in premodern

India, this concept is inadequate. Besides the fact that it excludes by definition the culture of the urban nonelite groups, it assumes a relatively simple structure which is essentially distinct from the high culture of the "Great Tradition". The concept, so defined, is an accurate statement of a *part*, but not the *totality*, of the culture of the common people. In the earlier stages of the development of the two Traditions, it is probably valid to say that they were essentially discrete systems of which the "Little Tradition" was marked by a basic simplicity of content. In later stages, in fact, probably for all documented periods of history, the culture of the common people included fully integrated ideas and institutions of great complexity, party developed at the level of the "Little Tradition", partly absorbed with suitable modifications from the higher culture. Moreover, the culture of the rural and urban masses was not essentially local or parochial, but characterized by a widespread homogeneity. In these respects, the long time period involved in the propagation of the culture performed a function comparable in its effectiveness to the modern mass media: a very wide circle was reached and large numbers absorbed the same ideas and institutions.

The culture of these large masses had elements of great complexity. The "Little Tradition" was both a part of the total culture and a culture unto itself for relatively small nonliterate groups (i.e., groups who were not only nonliterate themselves but were largely outside the influence of the purveyors of the literary traditions) about whom the only evidence available is in the survival of their counterparts down to contemporary times. In view of these facts, the culture of the masses in classical civilizations in premodern times requires some special term to distinguish it from the "Little Tradition", on the one hand, and the modern mass culture on the other. Perhaps "Popular Culture" describes adequately the somewhat imprecise concept involved.

The concrete expressions of the popular culture in medieval Bengal are to be found in a fairly copious literary effort, religious movements, a system of values, and a state of feelings which are strongly emphasized in the religions and literary works of the period. In the relatively meagre relics of artistic activity which have survived, there is a mixture of hieratic and folk elements, but even the basic spadework on this aspect of historical documentation remains to be done (except for some scholarly studies of medieval temples) and hence any discussion of this very important aspect of culture will not be attempted in this paper.

Each of the features of medieval Bengali culture mentioned above had its elite, as well as popular, facets and in many specific instances the line of demarcation was not very clear. It might be convenient, therefore, to first identify the elements which were distinctly elite and nonpopular in character. The specifically elite aspects of cultural activity were marked, in the first place, by the use of Sanskrit and, to a lesser extent, of Persian and Arabic. These were not the exclusive vehicles of elite culture, but where languages other than Bengali were used, the masses of unlettered people were automatically excluded. Language was something more than a vehicle of expression. It was the major link with the "Great Tradition" and fostered both imitative and creative interests in the particular contents of that tradition. *Nyaya* and *navya-nyaya, smrti, rasasastra*, religious treatises, court poetry of a highly stylized variety, were the main concern of the Sanskritic tradition in medieval Bengal, but there was also a thin stream of output in other branches of classical learning.

There is no detailed study yet of Perso-Arabic scholarship in medieval Bengal. We only know that urban elite groups, both Hindu and Muslim, acquired a knowledge of these languages, surely in the eighteenth century and probably earlier, and that there was a certain quantity of religious-literary output around the Sufi tradition. There were identifiably elite elements in Bengali works, but it is not easy to distinguish these from the heavily intermixed alloy of popular culture. To give a few examples, the writings of Alaol in the seventeenth century, and Bharatchandra in the eighteenth were meant to cater to highly sophisticated court audiences. Despite his religion, Alaol's diction is heavily Sanskritic, and he records his not-too-modest claims to the knowledge of several languages. Passages in his texts were surely incomprehensible to the unlettered. Similarly, Sundar's famous puns on his deity and his mistress obviously assumed in the audience a knowledge of Sanskrit literary conventions. Yet, the bulk of these literary works was not essentially different from the larger body of contemporary literature. Not only would these be comprehensible to the common people, but they contained characters and tales obviously derived from their lives. To appreciate how much closer these were to the traditions of popular culture, one has only to compare them with the literary works in classical Sanskrit, wherein the life of the common people appears, if at all, only as a backdrop for the life of the elite.

Even in the religious works of the period, one comes across items with a strong elitist bias. Chaitanya's famous biography of Krisna-das Kaviraj is permeated by the author's deep erudition, and the more popular writing of Vrindavan Das freely quotes the *Bhagavata* to confound the critics of Nityananda. Both these works are aimed, nevertheless, at "all men down to the Chandala".

The religious movements themselves reflected the differences in life style and the distinction between the "high" and the "low", the *uchcha* and the *nich jati*. The society of the respectable Vaishnava, whose life was regulated by Shritis cast in orthodox molds was out of bounds to the *Jat Boshtom*, the Vaishnava "caste" which grew out of the absorption of lower castes into the movement and was characterized by a relatively greater degree of freedom in religious beliefs and social practice.

The dominant theme of popular culture was religion interpreted in a very wide, nearly all-pervasive sense. This distinguished the popular culture from the elite, which was not unconcerned with religion, but placed a different emphasis upon it. The central focus of elite culture was not religion as the term is commonly understood. Whereas its popular counterpart was almost exclusively concerned with *bhakti* in one form or another the chief pride of the medieval Bengali intellect was *Nyaya* and *Smrti;* the latter was primarily an instrument for the preservation of the orthodox order, rather than a vehicle of religiosity. Even the emotionally exuberant Vaishnavism had to devise its *Smrti* and develop a *Rasasastra* along the lines of a very secular Sanskrit poetics, in order to find total acceptance with the elite.

Outside a very limited quantity of "court poetry", medieval Bengali literature — mostly the work of rural poets and very much a part of the life of the masses — is marked by a rare paucity of purely secular themes. The *padavalis* are mystical lyrics inspired by the loves of Krishna and Radha, the *panchalis* or *mangala-kavyas* sing the glories of particular deities, and the Vaishnava biographies spread the message of a god-man and his followers. The life and preoccupations of the poor villagers are woven into these literary texts, giving them their chief secular dimension and establishing at the same time a sense of affinity between the deity and the devotee. *Bhakti* becomes indistinguishable from family affection. The gods and goddesses of the *mangala-kavyas* were local deities who sought to be elevated to the highest heavens of the Hindu pantheon. In telling their tales, the poets introduce the great gods themselves as characters in the drama. The treatment, however, is very different from that of the Puranic myths. The *mangala-kavyas* are no mere narratives of marvellous happenings. Even great Siva is cast in the image of a poor peasant, sharing the miseries typical of his devotees' fate.

Religion, in the popular culture of medieval Bengal, thus acquired a very special character, becoming indistinguishable from the purely secular aspects of life. The "ballads" in praise of the supernatural powers personified as deities are meant to secure their favors, so that the course of a materially difficult existence is made a little smoother. But they become comprehensible as objects of *bhakti* — deep attachment — only through the process of identification; the adoration of a distant impersonal deity had no appeal. Once the identification is complete, the gods are assimilated into the world of deep sentiments—parental, filial, or fraternal love—which permeates medieval Bengali culture and provides an element of continuity with its modern counterpart. This absorption into a world of domestic sentiments characterizes Krittivasa's translation of the *Ramayana* and even the more Sanskritic translation of the *Mahabharata* by Kasiram Das. In the latter work, Vidura's great banquet in honor of Krishna becomes the offer of a few morsels of broken rice. Since Vidura was virtuous, to the poor Bengali translator of the great epic he was almost by definition hopelessly poor and his devotion to the incarnate Lord could be marked only by utter humility. The development of the Chaitanya legend, the transformation of man into God, is very much a part of this process of identification. Since God is man — "The son of our house" — the deification of a human being in one's own time becomes doubly convincing. The Master is accepted not only because he is proved to be God through miracles and revelations, but because the objects of worship had always been pictured as near and dear ones in the popular imagination. In the Vaishnava biographies, the Saint is not only the performer of marvellous acts as an incarnation of the deity, he is also the beloved child, full of pranks — but this too was an image familiarized by the legends of the child Krishna.

Religion in its more ostensible forms — popular religious movements and a variety of esoteric cults — was among the major preoccupations of the popular culture. In the background of Bengali literature there was a wide spectrum of obscure cults discussed authoritatively in S. B. Dasgupta's classic work on the subject. It is a remarkable fact that these diverse systems had a common stock of complex beliefs and practices which may be summed up as a faith in the possibility of transcendence through a specific set of practices: *deha-tatva* (mystical notions of the human physiology derived from *yoga* in one form or another); the *guru;* and the manipulation of the possible relationships between man and woman as a lever in the attainment of mystical experience, the ultimate object of all these cults. Thus the apparent diversity of esoteric cults did not imply any real fragmentation of popular culture.

The religious life of the Hindu masses was dominated by three coexisting elements — the worship of numerous deities, the Vaishnava movement, and Tantra. In fact, these three dominant elements of Bengali religious life bound together the elite and nonelite groups. Certain differences, however, need to be emphasized. The folk deities glorified in the *panchalis* might have been worshipped by all and sundry, but their worship was predominantly popular in origin and represented an impact of the "Little Tradition" on the "Great", the worship of the snake-goddess, for instance, being sanctified by a Sanskrit text. On the other hand the worship of Durga-Chandi might have had its origin in the folk tradition in remote antiquity, but it had been so fully incorporated in the Puranic "Great Tradition" of *Sakti* worship for centuries that in the Bengali Middle Ages it was in no sense predominantly a part of the popular culture alone. It had become integrated with elite culture in a way that the worship, for instance, of the personified diseases or village deities never did. Similarly, in the Vaishnava movement, while the first flush of charisma appears to have temporarily obliterated distinctions of caste and class, these soon reasserted themselves and the low caste *Jat Boshtom* went back through the *Sahajiva* beliefs and practices to the wider world of esoteric cults. This schematization, however, does not apply to Tantra, which both in its esoteric and household varieties reveals a centuries-old amalgam of highly intellectual and simplistic folk traditions. Significantly, all available texts on Tantra from medieval Bengal are written in Sanskrit, and the authors are all Brahmins. On the other hand, the *abhicharas* described in them are techniques for acquiring miraculous powers based on the crudest beliefs in magic and the supernatural. These have little to do with the high mystic purpose of the Tantric practices and are really related to the beliefs in magic and the supernatural which permeated medieval Bengali literature and even penetrated the austere and reputed *Smrti* work of Raghunandana. A further reason why Tantric cults do not fit easily into our scheme is that one cannot link the different levels of Tantric practices to different social strata of practitioners.

There are two elements in the popular culture of Bengal whose origins in time are not known, the ballads and the *rup-katha* (loosely translatable as fairy tales). The specific forms in which these are available may date back only to the nineteenth or the eighteenth century, but their origins almost certainly have claims to much greater antiquity. The distinctive character of these two literary genres consists in their purely secular content. Their links with the other forms of popular culture are to be found in the elusive area of feelings — a mood of pathos and emotionalism and a deep attachment to domestic ties. The quality of nearly fragile sensitiveness one encounters in the other literary forms reaches its acme here.

The cultural expressions discussed so far have certain affinities, with contemporary mass culture. The major components of Medieval popular culture, though available in literary forms, were communicated more directly to large groups over wide areas. And since this process went on for a long period of time, the same myths and ideas were transmitted to large masses of men, thereby imposing a pattern of homogeneity. The *panchalis*, subdivided into "palas" or plays, were publicly sung or produced as a dramatic performance. Some of the best-known works of this genre actually mention the particular days of the week on which the different sections were produced. The ballads and *rup-kathas* were mostly reconstructed in the twentieth century from orally transmitted traditions. The Vaishnava movement was propagated among the masses by missionaries, and the technique of *samkirtana*, ecstatic chanting in public, was a potent instrument in its dissemination. Thus although differences in technology make direct comparisons ludicrous, the remarkable uniformity in the beliefs and assumptions underlying the variety of individual practices, and the similarity of style and diction of literary works produced in different parts of the region which are known to have had different colloquial dialects, brought about a popular culture not unlike its modern counterpart in scope. Communication in Medieval Bengal became possible between distinct social, regional, and even communal groups, much as it is today.

The mass culture of modern Bengal, despite its strongly urban and commercialized character, has even more direct ties with its medieval past. The most popular festivals, both urban and rural, celebrated with the assistance of modern technology and typically modern institutions — phonographs, radio, trucks, neon signs, local clubs, etc. — are the worships of the mother goddess in her distinctly medieval forms. The notorious sentimentality of the popular Bengali film and fiction — I do not mean the more highbrow specimens — has its roots in an older emotionalism, though the mass media may represent a cruder level of sensibility. Even the possibility that the factionalism of leftist politics is a projection to a different environment of the intra-caste disputes Mukundaram described, may be less bizarre than it sounds.

10

SITALA AND THE ART OF PRINTING: THE TRANSMISSION AND PROPAGATION OF THE MYTH OF THE GODDESS OF SMALLPOX IN RURAL WEST BENGAL[1]

RALPH W. NICOLAS

In contemporary rural Bengal, myths[2] and other important social and religious information are communicated in three principal ways: orally, in manuscripts, and in printed books. Anthropological and folklore studies place great value upon the oral tradition — the handing down of narratives orally

1. The field research on which this paper is based was conducted under the support of a Fulbright-Hays Center Faculty Fellowship awarded through the South Asia Language and Area Center at Michigan State University. I am grateful for this support and to the Asian Studies Center and the Department of Anthropology for facilitating this work in many ways. I would also like to record my debt to my co-worker, Mr. Tarasish Mukhopadhyay, and to my wife Marta who collaborated in the fieldwork. Mr. Mukhopadhyay was able to check some of the statements made in a draft of this paper against his own extensive knowledge and to interview again some of the performers of the *Sitala-mangal* whom we know. He has corrected a number of errors of fact and interpretation that I made earlier and I am grateful to him. Professor A. K. Ramanujan kindly read and commented on the draft, making helpful suggestions and supplying me with a copy of his still unpublished paper on a topic closely related to this one. The approach that I have taken here is strongly influenced by the ideas laid out by Milton Singer (1958) in his introduction to the volume on *Traditional India: Structure and Change,* as well as by the contributions of Hein, McCormack, Raghavan, and Singer to that volume. Marriott's (1959) analysis of "Changing channels of cultural transmission in Indian civilization" has been similarly influential.

2. The term "myth" in this paper follows the customary Western conception rather than the Bengali, which draws finer distinctions among narratives of this general class than we are accustomed to make. Percy Cohen (1969: 337) characterizes myth in a practically useful way when he says

from generation to generation. Myths and tales learned by an old man years ago at the knee of his aged grandmother, by an adept of some cult, or by an initiate into a secret society are frequently recorded by anthropologists and folklorists for fear that they will soon disappear entirely. Certainly, here is a distinct romantic satisfaction to find oneself the first to have recorded a particular myth or tale; how much more so if one is the last.

Oral transmission and direct learning are the most ancient means by which the continuity of human cultures has been maintained; they are also, in many respects, the least efficient and the most likely to give way to improved methods of preservation and transmission. Although the oral tradition in India, clearly embodied in the *guru*-disciple relationship, has occupied a place of importance alongside the literary tradition, anthropologists have done relatively little in this field. Major emphasis in the study of Indian mythology has been philological, with the manuscript as the basic source. However, in contemporary rural West Bengal, neither the manuscript nor the oral tradition is as important a means of transmitting myths as is the inexpensive printed book.

The distinction between the "transmission" and the "propagation" of a myth that I make here is particularly important in a society such as that of Bengal in which specialization is the rule. I use the term "transmission" to refer to the processes by which myths are communicated from one generation to the next — to their cultural preservation. In rural Bengal, the transmission of myths is primarily the task of specialists who are necessarily concerned with the completeness,

---

A myth is a narrative of events; the narrative has a sacred quality; the sacred communication is made in symbolic form; at least some of the events and objects which occur in the myth neither occur nor exist in the world other than that of the myth itself; and the narrative refers in dramatic form to origins or transformations. The narrative quality distinguishes a myth from a general idea or set of ideas, such as a cosmology. The sacred quality and the reference to origins or transformations distinguish myth from legend and other types of folk-tale. The narration of events and reference to objects unknown outside the world of myth differentiates myth from history or pseudo-history.

detail, and accuracy of the narratives that they control. Virtually everyone in the society knows the general outlines of the most common myths, but the specialists require full knowledge. By "propagation" I mean the processes by which myths are communicated to and re-inforced in the minds of most members of the society.[3] In rural Bengal, those who propagate the myth are also specialists; thus, propagation is primarily communication from specialists to the nonspecialist public. There is some overlap between these processes, even where specialization is marked. In a less differentiated society than that of rural Bengal, there might be nearly complete identity between the two processes, with transmission taking place almost exclusively in the context of propagation.

Like most culturally significant tasks in Indian society, reading and writing themselves were specialist functions until comparatively recent times. The British conception of education and the demands of the modern job and marriage markets resulted in the fact that nearly half the men and about an eighth of the women in the rural area that I shall be discussing are "literate". Among them only a portion can read a religious text. Moreover, among the owners of religious texts, it is likely that a majority do not read them and have never read them; these books (and, in a few cases, manuscripts) lie in bundles before family shrines, where they are worshipped along with the family deities. However, among the specialists in the transmission and propagation of myths, I have seen a few well-worn books that have performed their functions many times over.

In this paper, I shall be concerned with the transmission and propagation of myth in a cluster of eight villages, collectively known as "Kelomal", located in the Tamluk Subdivision of Midnapur District, West Bengal. There are, of course, many parts of rural India in which rates of effective literacy are even lower and where printed books are even less commonly available than in this area. Nonetheless, I believe cer-

---

3. Goody and Watt (1963: 326) make a distinction similar to the one that I propose between "transmission" and "propagation"; they contrast the "processes of collective development and transmission" to the "process of transmission from one individual to another."

Sitala and the Art of Printing

tain generalizations concerning the effects of media upon the transmission and propagation of myths are valid.

Sitala

A goddess who is thought to control smallpox, and often, a variety of other contagious diseases, is found in almost every part of India. She goes by a wide variety of names in the South;[4] but she is generally called *Sitala*, or something derived from it, in the North. Most deities who are as widely worshipped as the smallpox goddess(es) make an early appearance in Indian religious literature and, if their names are not to be found in the Vedic corpus, undergo a personality syncretism with some Vedic deity. However, as best as I can determine, *Sitala* — with whom I am principally concerned here — appears only twice in brief passages in Sanskrit works of late composition: the *Picchila Tantra*, a work of such obscurity that it does not even merit mention in Kane's *History of Dharmasastra*, and the *Skanda Purana*, a late, largely derivative work (Bhattacharya 1952: 56; Banerjea 1956: 24-25; Mukhopadhyaya 1965: 453-55).[5]

In Northern and Central India, *Sitala* appears primarily in the oral tradition;[6] only in Bengal, so far as I have been able to discover, is there a substantial vernacular literature devoted

---

4. Whitehead (1921: 30-31) says that while *Mariamma*, the Tamil smallpox goddess and villages mother, has won her "way to general respect or fear among the Tamil people," in the Telugu country, "as a rule the infliction and removal of epidemics and disasters is a general function of all goddesses alike."

5. Asutos Bhattacarya (1964: 723) says that the *stava of Sitala* is also found in the second section, fourth part, of the *Bhavaprakasa*, a Ayurvedic medical text, as a part of the cure for smallpox. This work appears to be, at the earliest, sixteenth century (Chakraberty 1923: 419), since it describes syphilis as *phiranga roga*, the "Portugese disease." Bhanj Deo (1954: 1) cites a reference to *Sitala* in the *Brhadyogin Tantra*, where she appears as the benign form of the *Yogini Pisitasana*. The skull-cap (or severed head) and knife carried by the *Yogini* are exchanged for the pot of nectar and the brooom of *Sitala*. Both forms have the ass as a vehicle.

6. Crooke's (1968: 125-136) discussion of *Sitala* in North India does not suggest that there is any literary authority for her worship and indicates that there is a great deal of diversity in beliefs concerning her.

to her. This literature belongs to a distinctively Bengali class called *mangal-kavya*, which is primarily narrative interspersed with lyrical passages. Edward Dimock (1963:6) characterizes it as "village poetry" and says

> The legends which the *mangal* poems contain are old; though few of the poems themselves seem to be earlier than the fifteenth century, it is certain that they were passed down orally over many centuries before being put by a particular writer into the form in which we have them today. The dating of a particular version of the poem does not necessarily reflect the dating of the legend itself. (p. 197).

Most of the poems of the *mangal* class, which go by a variety of Bengali names, are myths that eulogize particular gods and goddesses and relate their careers, particularly their dealings with mortal men and the establishment of their worship on earth. Some of them concern deities well-known all over South Asia and in ancient Sanskrit literature — *Laksmi* and *Saraswati*, for example. Some deal with gods and goddesses, such as *Jagannath* and *Candi*, known all over India but of primarily regional importance. The most interesting of these, however, are the *mangals* of purely Bengali divinities: *Manasa*, the goddess of snakes; *Daksin Ray*, the tiger god; *Sasthi*, who is responsible for the welfare of children; and *Dharma*, the white god. The *Sitala-mangal* belongs to this latter category. Although *Sitala* is known throughout the Indo-European speaking portions of South Asia by a name closely resembling that in Bengali and is generally associated with smallpox and other contagious diseases, the myth of the *Sitala-mangal* seems to be peculiarly Bengali and the personality attributed to her in it is apparently not established elsewhere.

Some of the *mangal* poems have proved exceptionally valuable to students of social history (e.g., Inden 1967, Dimock and Inden 1969) because they contain such clear representations of their authors' conceptions of the social order. Others have received the attention of historians of religion, because of the insight they provide into ancient and obscure religious belief and practice; or of philologists, because of the archaism of their language. Some of the *mangal-kavyas* have attracted scholars of literature because of the artistic merit of their poetry. The various versions of the *Sitala-mangal*, however, have not received much attention from any scholars: they contain little information of historical importance, are mostly of relatively recent composition, are highly imitative of earlier *mangals* in style and content, and, generally, little can be said for them as literature.

The defects of the *Sitala-mangal*, from the perspectives of scholars in other disciplines, create awkward problems for an anthropologist. It would have been most useful to have had a collaborator in the field of Bengali language and literature with competence in the literary manifestation of the goddess. Nevertheless, I have undertaken the study of both the village *Sitala* and the *Sitala* of the *mangal-kavya*, since the people among whom I worked consider her in both forms.

SITALA-MANGAL

Dimock, quoted earlier, mentions that the myths that appear in *mangal* poetry forms were doubtless transmitted orally prior to their having been written down. The four manuscript versions of the *Sitala-mangal* about which I know something are clearly derived from different, although connected, oral traditions.[7] The earliest written version of the *Sitala* myth appears to be that of one Daivakinandan (who calls himself Kavi Vallabha) who lived in Burdwan District and wrote during the early part of the seventeenth century (Bhattacharya 1952:62; D. C. Sen 1954:321). The two "dramas" (*pala*) in his poem are quite different stories from those known to me. The second version is a minor work among a long series of *mangal* poems composed by Krsnaram Das who lived in a village just to the North of Calcutta; it dates from about

---

7. Tarapada Bhattacarya (1962: 172) mentions the existence of four other manuscript versions of the *Sitala-mangal,* composed by "Dayal," Akincan Cakrabarti, "Dvijagopala," and "Sankara." Tamonas Candra Das Gupta (1951:200) mentions versions by "Ramprasad" (Sen?), "Krsnanath" (=Krsnaram Das?), "Sankaracaryya" (=Sankara?), and "Raghunath Datta." This last is the name of one of the *palas* of the Kavivallabh version, according to Asutosh Bhattacarya (1952: 62).

1690[8]. The other two versions, those of Manikram Ganguli and Nityananda Cakravarti, are of late eighteenth century composition (S.Sen 1960: 140-144). Manikram was a poet of the Rarh country; Nityananda lived in the deltaic eastern portion of Midnapur district. It is this latter area and Nityananda's version of the myth that concern me most.

Nityananda was a courtier of the Raja of Kasijora Pargana, named Rajnarayan, whose age, Asutosh Bhattacharya (1952: 66-67) tells us, "cannot be known".[9] However, as a Bengali *zamindar*, Raja Rajnarayan's name could not fail to appear in connection with a land dispute, in the course of one of which one Kasinath Babu, Security of his estates, tells us that he inherited his father's *zamindari* estate in 1756-57 and died without a legitimate heir in 1770-71 (Sengupta and Bose 1962: 24-26). Thus, the text is clearly dated.

Raghunathbari, the capital of Kasijora Pargana, lies about seven miles northwest of a group of villages called Kelomal in which I did fieldwork in 1968-69 and about six miles west of villages in which I worked in 1960-61. One of these latter villages, which I have called Govindapur, was a part of Kasijora Pargana; it was in Govindapur that I first saw and heard a performance of the *Sitala-mangal*. Like four public performances of the myth that I witnessed in 1969, the 1960 performances were by men of the locality who are specialists of some repute: they are hired by villages and neighborhoods all over the deltaic portion of southwestern Bengal to perform for them. They travel to villages in Howrah and Hooghly Districts and in the deltaic portions of their home district, Midnapur. In addition, they are often hired by organizations sponsoring neighbourhood *pujas* for *Sitala* in Calcutta. *Sitala* seems to be less important in the villages lying to the west of the delta margin, in western Midnapur and Bankura Districts. Thus, I think that there is a relatively clear territory

---

8. This version consists of three *palas: Madan Das Jagatir Pala, Kajir Pala,* and *Hrsikes Sadhur Upakhyana* (Satyanarayana Bhattacarya 1958: lxxvii, 251-285).

9. Later, quoting an article by Byamokesh Mustaphi, Asutosh Bhattacarya (1964: 734) suggests that Rajnarayana may have been a "powerful" but "book-loving" *zamindar* dated about 1777 or 1783 A.D.

Sitala and the Art of Printing

over which there may be broad similarities in the myth and cult of *Sitala;* I may have accidentally selected something near the religious center of the territory as the site of my field research.[10]

The Goddess

Sitala's dhyana-mantra, taken from the *Picchila Tantra,* describes her as being of white complexion, sitting on an ass, holding a broom resting on a full pitcher of water from which she sprinkles life-giving water by means of the broom, naked, with a winnowing fan on her head, ornamented with gold and jewels, three-eyed and mitigating the terrible suffering of skin eruptions. A similar description is contained in her *stotram,* taken from her *Skanda Purana* (Mukhopadhyay 1965: 553-55; Bhattacharyya 1952:56). It is in this form, (although not naked, but dressed as a married woman), seated side-saddle fashion on her *vahana,* the ass, that she is most commonly represented by the potters who make images for neighborhood *pujas* in Calcutta. Such images are established at convenient outdoor locations during the hot, dry weather of May and June, immediately preceding the monsoon. The goddess is worshipped both by a Brahman priest and in a public performance; then she is either immersed in some body of water, or her spirit is released from the image by the immersion mantra, the lifeless image being allowed to stand where it is, giving a kind of second-class *darsan* to passers-by.

Representations of *Sitala* found in the villages of Kelomal have little evident connection with the anthropomorphic figures of Calcutta or with the goddess described in the *dhyana-mantra* or *stotram.* In Kelomal and the surrounding area, the image of the goddess may be made of stone, metal, or

---

10. Binay Ghos (1957: 405) writes: *"Sitala Devi's* outstanding popularity is visible in the Contai, Tamluk, and Ghatal areas [of Midnapur District]. The *Sitala pujas* of almost all parts of Bengal were introduced [from there]. At the time of smallpox and cholera epidemics, the grand celebration of her special *puja* is to be seen. I think that *Sitala* is said to be the foremost among village deities in the areas of Contai, Tamluk, and Ghatal. The public worship of *Sitala* is the foremost festival of the villages and it is celebrated [there] with the greatest pomp of all."

pottery. There are some figurines of brass, mostly modern, that are fully anthropomorphic but that lack any obvious characteristics that might distinguish them from a variety of other goddesses; this is true of the baked pottery representations also, although these seem to be usually older then the brass images.

Stone is not native to the Bengal delta and stone working is not an art for which this area is famous. Stone images of *Sitala* are usually crudely shaped. One that I know of amounts to no more than a rough sphere with a slightly raised nose and slightly depressed areas corresponding to eyes. A locally renowned goddess, from the nearby vilage of Mahisali, has a brass face with cowry shells for eyes, and a nose and tongue made of sheet silver; her entire face is studded with silver pustules.[11] The stone form in which she originally appeared is concealed behind a silver breast-plate. She has detachable silver hands and legs.

Most of these figures are heavily coated with vermilion (sindur), giving them a crimson complexion quite unlike the white one described in her *mantras;* however, in the case of vegetarian *Sitalas,* the image is sometimes allowed to remain the color of the material from which it is manufactured. She is invariably dressed as a married woman in red cloth or a red-bordered sari.

Vegetarianism is only one of the characteristics in which the *Sitalas* of different villages vary one from another; each goddess of standing has a reputation for distinct personality characteristics, likes and dislikes. There are separate, although similar, myths concerning the origin of many images; most of these are as frequently called "Mother of such-and-such village" as they are called *Sitala.* Thus, while *Sitala* remains

---

11. These pustules are called, in euphemistic reversal, *tikli,* "cosmetic ornaments." *Tikli* is derived from *tika,* "religious" or "sectarian mark," such as are often placed on the foreheads of Hindu worshippers; *tika* also means "vaccination mark." Innoculation with live smallpox virus was practiced indigenously in rural Bengal, primarily upon young children, prior to the introduction of the Jennerian vaccine; *Sitala* was invoked in connection with the innoculation (Buchanan — Hamilton 1807-08, Book II, "The People").

the goddess of smallpox, she is also the *gram-Candi* for most villages in or near Kelomal. Not all villages, however, have a permanent image of *Sitala;* and not all villages that have permanent images have public temples to house them or agricultural land set aside to support them. Where villages do not have images of the goddess, the common village *Sitala puja* is done *ghat sthapana*, that is, by invoking the deity into a specially prepared earthen pot, which is immersed at the end of the ceremony.

Sitala is never worshipped alone. At minimum she is accompanied by her companion, *Jvarasur*,[12] the Fever Demon, and by her serving woman *Raktabati*, who receive worship secondary to that which *Sitala* receives. Where there is a village temple for the goddess, it often also houses other deities, such as *Manasa*, the goddess of snakes, who cannot be ignored when worship is given to *Sitala*, although the worship of other gods and goddesses is clearly secondary to that given the village mother. There is, however, one deity whose worship is essential when a village *Sitala puja* is held: she is *Olabibi*,[13] the

---

12. Gopendrakrsna Basu (1969: 72-75) reports that *Jvarasur* is "not only *Sitala's;* he appears in some villages as the chief minister of *Pancananda* [a terrible, disease-related form of Siva] and as the companion of *Dharmathakur.*" He is also sometimes worshipped independently. Occasionally, he is represented as having "three heads, nine eyes, six hands, and three legs."

13. Gopendrakrsna Basu (1969: 25-28), in his chapter on *Olaicandi*, asserts that *Olaicandi* is generally the name of the goddess of cholera in the Hindu- majority areas. This generalization obviously does not apply to the eastern part of Midnapur District, in which the Hindu *Mahisya* caste constitutes a majority of the population and where, even before 1947, Muslims were a relatively small minority. I have heard some Hindus refer to the goddess as *Oladevi;* I attribute this to a heightened consciousness of religious differences, which is also manifested in the critical attitude that some Muslims take toward the worship of *Olabibi* by their coreligionists. In his chapter on *Olabibi* (pp. 185-190), Basu notes that this goddess is found in virtually all of the villages in the southern part of Twenty-four Parganas District. Basu says that there is a middle Bengali text called *Satbibir Gan* (Song of the Seven Bibis) and that *Olabibi* often appears as one of seven sisters, similar to the popular Hindu *Saptamatrka* (Seven Mother Goddess). However, where a shrine is hers alone, he says, "priesthood is most commonly done by Muslim fakirs," as is the case in eastern Midnapur. See also Hora (1933).

Muslim goddess of cholera. There are, for practical purposes, no Muslims in any of the eight Kelomal villages. Puja is given to *Olabibi* by a Muslim priest from a neighboring community on behalf of the village that is holding the ceremony. While not so much time or money is devoted to the worship of *Olabibi* as is given to *Sitala*, her *puja* is clearly of some importance.

Olabibi is represented aniconically on an outdoor shrine.[14] In the Kelomal villages, this is usually built of brick plastered with cement and consists of a set of three steps, altogether about two feet high and three feet across, topped by three mounds side by side. Some villages do not have such a permanent shrine but construct one out of mud a few days before the *puja*. In other villages, the cement holding the bricks together has decayed and these are put back together with fresh mud in advance of the ceremony. In nearby villages, some of the *Olabibi* shrines have four pillars situated on a high mound or under a small arched roof. None of the local *Olabibis* has a particular reputation or distinct personality; there is, however, one in a village near Raghunathbari, the capital of Kasijora Pargana, who is held in great repute, and her shrine is maintained year-round by the Patidar (or Patuya) caste, in whose neighborhood it is located. I shall return to a consideration of *Olabibi* in connection with her myths.

The Myth

The reason that only the version of the *Sitala-mangal* written by Nityananda Cakravarti will be considered here has already been stated. And I shall deal only with the edition published by Tarachand Das and Sons of Calcutta, which is the edition used by performers of this myth whom I know. This edition first appeared in 1931; however, on the back of the title page,

---

14. I have used the word "shrine" to translate the rustic Bengali word *than*. Basu (1969: 193) rightly, I think, says that it is misleading to connect this word with *sthan*, which simply means "place," since *than* means the "temple of a popular deity" although "no villager calls it a temple *(mandir).*" He describes the ordinary *than* as being simply an earthen platform at the base of a tree, which is accurate for the Kelomal area except in respect of *Olabibir thans*, which I describe.

we are informed that "this book was originally published in 1285 *sal* (1878-79) by Binodbihari Sil in the Manik Library.. Now we hold exclusive rights." It seems, then, that Nityananda's work was printed a little more than a century after he wrote it, an interesting fact in view of the complete absence of "modern" content in the work, the ferment that was taking place in Bengali intellectual life in Calcutta at the time of its publication, and the significant advance that Western education had made in Bengal by that time. Moreover, the edition of Taracad Das and Sons has gone through at least twelve printings; while I do not know the size of those printings, it is clear that many thousands of copies are in circulation and have been in the last ninety years. I mention these facts in order to indicate that while it is a rustic narrative with which I am concerned, it is one that has been of interest to some millions of people over the last two centuries! I give here only a brief summary of the myth of *Sitala* as written by Nityananda; I hope to provide a full translation in the near future.

Nityananda's *Sitala-mangal* begins with the birth of the goddess and progresses through a series of episodes called *palas*. The word *pala* most commonly means "turn" (as when village families take monthly turns in offering food at the common village Visnu temple), but in this case it means a kind of drama. Performers of the myth assert that they can divide the entire story into ten separate *palas* to be performed on ten successive nights. They are rarely called upon to do this; most villages cannot afford to hire them for more than two nights and most lay primary emphasis upon one night, on which the performance is carried on until it is nearly dawn. The audience watching such a performance is thought to be keeping a vigil (*jagaran*) for the goddess; the devotion thus displayed is regarded as generally meritorious. The entire *mangal* poem is subtitled *Sitalar jagaran pala*, "The Drama of the Vigil of Sitala." The largest *pala* in the myth is the *Birat pala*, in which *Sitala* humbles the great King of Birat and makes him her worshipper.[15] There are many sub-

---

15. The Birat Raja of the *Sitala-mangal* seems to be the same character

ordinate *palas* within the *Birat pala* so that it can be expanded and contracted in performance and the subordinate *palas* may be performed on separate nights.

Sitala was born from the cooled remains of the fire in which the heavenly King Nahusa offered a sacrifice in order to obtain a son. She appeared as a beautiful young woman with a winnowing fan on her head. *Brahma*, the Creator, asked who she was, and she said that she did not know. Therefore, he named her *Sitala*, "The Cool One," because she had been born from the cool ashes of the sacrificial fire.[16] He directed her to go to the land of mortal men, where she would be worshipped as a goddess. He provided her with various kinds of lentils (which later become the means by which she gives pox to those who humiliate or reject her on earth). She requested two boons from *Brahma* before she began her earthly adventure: that her worship first be performed in heaven, so that mortals would know how to do it, and that she be given a companion. *Brahma* sent her to *Siva* to present these requests. *Siva* created the mighty Fever Demon, *Jvarasur*, from the perspiration on his forehead. The Fever Demon so terrified the gods and goddesses that they asked *Visnu* to destroy him. *Visnu* sent his discus, which cut the monster in three parts and killed him; *Siva* restored him to life but left him with three heads, six arms, six legs, etc.

Sitala, dressed as an old Brahman woman, and with the terrific Fever Demon disguised as a child, went to the court of the mighty Indra. There she had to afflict all the gods and goddesses with smallpox and fever before they performed her *puja*. *Siva* told those who had insulted *Sitala* of the tragic error they had made; they immediately worshipped

---

as the Virat Raja of the Mahabharata; the principal queen and the chief minister both have identical names in the two narratives. Many events and names in Nityananda's version of the myth are evidently borrowed from the *Mahabharata*. The effect of such borrowing is probably to lend additional authority to the *Sitala* myth, but I cannot take up this problem here.

16. The origin attributed to *Sitala's* name in the myth should not, of course, be allowed to obscure its euphemistic reversal: She, whose affliction causes raging fever, is addressed as "The Cool One."

Sitala and became her devotees, whereupon all were cured of their various maladies.

Accompanied by the Fever Demon, the goddess began her adventures on earth, principally in the kingdom of Birat. She first appeared before the King, a devout Saivite, in a horrible dream containing explicit portents of the destruction to come if he did not worship her. This dream, however, did not break his single-minded devotion to *Siva*. There follows, in the narrative, a long interlude in which *Sitala* marshalled her resources, in the form of poxes and other communicable diseases of far greater variety than the Western taxonomist of pathologies can muster. Here also appear *Sitala's* vehicle, the ass, and her serving woman *Raktabati* (whose name is obviously related to *raktabati*, "she who possesses the blood," one of the names of smallpox).

Sitala's first confrontation in the kingdom of Birat was with a boatman named Nima, who insisted that she pay the fare for a ferry ride from her stock of lentils. She sent him home with some of her "peas of eternal life"; his sons found these exceptionally delectable, but six days after they had eaten them, they were seized with smallpox and died. Nima was on the point of taking his own life when *Sitala*, still in disguise, revealed herself to him and said that she could restore his sons to life. She turned their corpses to stone. Nima and his wife took the stone bodies home and, eventually, when the Birat Raja worshipped *Sitala*, they were restored to life.

Next, *Sitala* spread the devastation of her diseases throughout the entire kingdom, selling lentils in the markets. She killed the King's own sons, the last three of whom he made strenuous efforts to hide from her, and nine lakhs of his subjects. The King's principal wife, *Sudesna*, and his youngest son's wife remained devotees of *Sitala* throughout this period of trial. Eventually, the King offered worship to the goddess and *Sitala puja* was done, with blood sacrifices, in every house in the kingdom. The goddess then restored her victims to life.

In the next "drama" a *Sadhu* and physician from the Birat kingdom, Debdas Datta, at *Sitala's* command and under her protection, undertook a long journey to bring the goddess's golden pot to the Birat court. He visited a number of lands, both known (Vrndavana, Banaras, and Gaya) and imaginary Mayades and Pakisa. Finally, there is a short *pala* called *Gokul puja* in which the inhabitants of Gokul are humbled by the goddess, who saved *Krsna* and *Balaram* themselves from smallpox.

This is an outline of the *Sitala* myth as presented in the most commonly used printed text. In performance, some sections are expanded and embroidered upon, others are de-emphasized, and some are omitted entirely. Each group of specialist performers attempts to create a distinctive performance of the myth. Local references and the names of local persons are inserted in amusing contexts. And Vaisnava *Kirtans* that are appropriate in mood to various parts of the story are sung as a kind of interlude at many points, according to the length of performance desired. The basic line of the story and the specific actions related, however, are highly consistent from one performance to the next. By contrast with this consistency, I examine two versions of the *Olabibi* myth.

The Olabibi myth

The first version of the *Olabibi Gan* (song of *Olabibi*) that I relate was performed by a group under the leadership of Sri Kunja Bihari Nandi, and Utkal *sreni* Brahman of Amgechya village.

Narayan decided that he should have worshippers among Muslims as he did among Hindus and decided that the best way to manage this was to be born a Muslim. The Badshah's daughter lived a secluded life, as became a Muslim woman of high birth. She saw only her mother and a few courtiers, the sixteen serving women who constantly attended her, and her religious teacher who came regularly to read "kitab and Koran" to her. One day the teacher told her that she had heard all of the Muslim scriptures and that it would benefit her more to have a bath (*ghosal*) in a river. She asked her mother's permission to leave the palace for a bath. This was an alarming prospect but the mother consented with the provision that the entire path from the houses to the banks of the Yamuna be enclosed in cloth and that the sixteen serving women go with her.

The arrangements were made and the girls were playing in the water when a lotus came floating past. The lotus was *Narayan* himself, transformed by his *maya*, or power of illusion. The princess sniffed the lotus and, unknown to anyone, the seed of *Narayan* entered her body as the perfume of the flower. Later they returned to the palace and, as the days went by, it became increasingly clear to the princess that she was pregnant. First the serving women learned of this; then her mother found her crying and discovered her secret. Her mother questioned her closely but could find no connection with a man through which the girl might have become pregnant. The serving women urged the queen to arrange the girl's marriage as quickly as possible. The queen said that she had long been requesting the Badshah to give her in marriage but he thought that there was no groom suitable for his daughter.

The queen went to the Badshah and told him of their misfortune. He was shocked. She asked him again to arrange for the girl's marriage and criticized him for not having done it long ago. The Badshah summoned his chief minister (*ujir*) to discuss the problem. He proposed to the minister that he have the girl killed outright but the minister warned him of the great sin of killing women, Brahmans, and cows. The minister went to the princess and again questioned her closely. She told him the story of the lotus and also suggested that there might have been a man watching from a distance as she bathed. The minister discounted these possibilities and returned to the Badshah without any explanation of the mysterious pregnancy. The Badshah had become concerned about his reputation in his kingdom and asked the minister what he could do. The minister suggested that the princess be confined to prison with sentries and with thirty-two serving women to be with her constantly. "When the child is born, we can examine his face and determine which man it resembles; the father shall be punished with death," the minister concluded.

The scene is shifted to the prison. Narayan spoke to the princess from within her wormb. He requested that she give him a tiny piece of cloth with a small hole in it so that he might not be born naked. The princess was understandably astounded to hear a voice coming from her belly and told him of her unhappiness. He said, "Well, I know everything, but for the time being I need a small piece of cloth." She tore a piece from the end of her sari. Immediately, the labour pains began; the child was born but disappeared before the mother could even see it. (The performers here interposed the information that "this is *maya* [the illusory power of a deity], this is the *maya* of a god, this is the *maya* of Narayan.") Only a flower lay on the ground at the place of delivery.

The serving women immediately reported to the king the birth and strange disappearance of the princess's child. The furious king summoned his minister, upbraided him for having proposed the unsuccessful plan, and ordered him to take the princess into a jungle filled with wild animals where she would be killed. The minister did as he was ordered and abandoned the princess in the jungle without food or shelter. She began to lament: "Hai, Allah. I was raised in the seclusion of the *Zenana*. Now I am alone in the jungle surrounded by wild animals. Yet, I believe that I am free from sin." Immediately, *Olabibi* appeared and addressed her as "Dear mother." [Here, again, is the deity's *maya*, the male god Narayan appearing as the female *Olabibi*.] *Olabibi* described herself as the princess's child and told her that she could suffer no harm, even in so dangerous a place, because she was under the protection of *Olabibi*.

When the minister had left with the princess, *Olabibi* had struck down his son with cholera. *Olabibi* reappeared in the Badshah's court and told the minister that she could restore his son's life if he would worship her with an offering of *sirani*,[17] He quickly did this and the son was restored to life. The minister took to the Badshah some of the *prasad* of his offering to *Olabibi*. The Badshah enquired about the source of this *sirani* and the minister related the story of his meeting

17. *Sirani* (alternatively, *sirani*, or more commonly *sirni* or *sinni*) is an uncooked mixture of bananas, unboiled milk, wheat flour, molasses or sugar, and spices. It is thought to be an appropriate offering to Muslim saints.

with *Olabibi* and his son's restoration to life. The Badshah was contemptuous and said, "*Olabibi* is a goddess of the Bengalis and the beggars." The minister, however, said that he would continue to worship her.

Next, *Olabibi* presented herself to the Badshah; she asked him to worship her. He told her that he did not recognize her and demanded proof that she was the powerful goddess she claimed to be. "There is a *jagaddal pathar* [immovably heavy stone that weights down the universe] in our pilgrimage place at Mecca. That stone is suspended with no support. I would like you to show that stone to me here", the Badshah challenged her. Olabibi said that she would bring it to him and then instantly produced the stone. The Badshah acknowleged *Olabibi's* divine status, then asked her who she was and how she came there. She described herself as the child of his unmarried daughter. The Badshah then realized the significance of the earlier events and worshipped *Olabibi*. "From that time," the performers concluded, "the *puja* of *Olabibi* became prevalent in the *Kaliyuga*."

I relate a second version of the *Olabibi* myth principally in order to show the great variety among the several versions. This one was performed by a group from Ilka village in Mahishadal Thana under the direction of Sri Sakti Pada Misra, a Byasakta *sreni* Brahman. *Krsna* was standing beneath his heavenly *kadamba* tree when a *Raksasi* (anthropophagous demoness) appeared before him. She instantly resolved herself into four sisters, through her *maya*. They were *Ola* ("She who comes down," i.e., the discharge of the bowels in cholera), *Utha* ("She who comes up," i.e., the vomiting in cholera; *Olautha* together means cholera), *Hasan* (a smile), and *Campak* (the flower of a magnolia-like tree). *Krsna* asked the four sisters what work they would do. *Ola* said, "I will cause diarrhea and, together, *Olautha* will cause death." *Utha* said, "I will kill with a glance." *Hasan* said, "I will kill with a smile." And *Campak* said, "When I smile together with *Hasan*, all will be killed."

Krsna agreed that *Ola* and *Utha* could go into the world of mortal men but he required *Hasan* and *Campak* to remain behind. He told *Ola* and *Utha* that they might go wherever the name of *Hari* (*Visnu*) was not heard, but that they could not go where *Hari Nam Kirtan* was sung. He charged them to remember his command "in the name of Allah" (*allar dohai*) and said that this was Allah's wish but that no one would know of it except them.

Throughout the *Satyayuga*, the *Tretayuga*, and the *Dwaparayuga*, when men were religious, *Ola* and *Utha* could find no opportunities to use their destructive power. But in the present age (Kaliyuga), when:

> the institutions of caste do not remain
> and people don't respect their *gurus*;
> proper social distinctions do not remain.
> Then it will cease to rain,
> jackals will climb trees, tigers will give birth to goats,
> girls of the Oilpresser caste will become princesses
> and leather-workers will become kings;
> Hunters will become ministers
> and Candalas will carry the umbrellas of Brahmans.

In this age, *Ola* and *Utha* found employment. They went first to the Badshah and asked him to offer them worship. He refused to acknowledge their divinity. Then they went out into his kingdom; they found two cowherd boys playing in a field and offered them sweets containing the poison of cholera. The boys died immediately.

When the boys did not return home with the cattle, the parents began to follow the cattle tracks and found their two dead sons in the field. *Ola* and *Utha* appeared before the sorrowful parents and said that if the parents could obtain worship for them, they would restore their sons to life. The parents asked, "Who are you?" "We are *Olabibi*," the sisters said. "We can bring your sons back to life if the Badshah gives us *puja*." The parents went quickly to the Badshah and told him their story. The Badshah agreed that if *Olabibi* could restore the boys to life, then he would give her (or them) *puja*. The parents related this to *Olabibi*, who sprinkled a little water on the bodies of the boys, reanimating them. Then the Badshah, the parents, and all of the Badshah's subjects offered worship to *Olabibi*.

Sitala and the Art of Printing 171

The remarkable differences between these two versions of the creation and deeds of *Olabibi* are paralleled by considerable discrepancies in the identification of the mythical figures represented by the three (or four) mounds that stand atop the Olabibi shrines. People simply did not agree about the identities of these mounds; numerous conceptions were presented as authoritative. These discrepant versions of the *Olabibi* myth were recorded by hand in school note books; this, no doubt, is what remains of the Bengali manuscript (*puthi*) tradition in an age of cheap printing and widespread literacy. I shall return to the problem of discrepancy and coherence in mythology after considering the performances of these myths.

THE PROPAGATION OF THE MYTH

I have postponed explaining what is meant by the "performance of a myth" until this point because performance is a complex event and it is the myth rather than its presentation that primarily concerns me. Moreover, I am omitting entirely any consideration of the Brahmanical ritual that is performed along with the myth. The performance of *puja* to *Sitala* by a Brahman priest on behalf of the village is theoretically just as important as the performance of the myth. It is the performance of the myth, however, that excites public attention and that provides the principal stimulus for the organizing of the ceremony. The organization of a factionalized village to hold such a ritual, despite its obvious importance for the community, is a difficult problem and a fascinating example of an occasion in which high normative coherence embraces embattled camps and unites them in a common effort. All of these considerations will have to be left aside now, however, and I turn instead to the organization of the performing group which is hired by the village to present the myth to them.

What I have called "the performing group" is known as *sayal gan dal*. *Sayal* means something like "travelling about for pleasure", *gan* means "song," and *dal* means "party" or "group," so that the entire expression means approximately "a party of travelling singers"; it has a happy or positive connotation. What I have called the "performance" is known in the local idiom as *sayal gan*, and is a pleasurably anticipated occasion for all villagers, but especially for youngsters and women.

A *sayal gan* may go on for up to ten days. However, I have seen none longer than two days; most last only one, at least most did in 1969, after two or three years of especially bad crops. The expense involved in presenting *sayal gan* goes up rapidly when the performers stay for several days: not only do their fees rise proportionately, but they must be housed and fed at village expense. Although a contract is made with the entire *dal*, through its leader, for the performance desired, the cost is usually from Rs. 3 to Rs. 5 per member for an afternoon and evening's performance, plus a meal, breakfast, and *biris* to smoke. The *dals* that I saw ranged from ten to twenty-five members, so the total expenditure for this part of the ritual is very large from the perspective of a poverty-stricken Bengali villager.

Most of the members of the *dals* that I saw were Mahisyas, members of the numerically dominant agricultural caste of the locality; and so were most of the members of their audiences. Although she is equally "Mother" of all villagers, *Sitala* is most closely associated with the Mahisyas, and what are called "village affairs" are primarily Mahisya-organized and controlled, even in villages where other high-ranking castes are economically and politically dominant. A few members of some *dals* were caste Vaisnavas, and the leaders of two of the four *dals* were Brahmans, one of the Byasakta *sreni*, which does the household *pujas* of the Mahisyas, and the other of Utkal *sreni*, a group, said to originate in Orissa, that provides priests for some collective Mahisya ceremonies and cooks for major feasts where members of several different castes are to be fed. There were no members of high-ranking Brahman or Kayastha castes in any of these groups.

Sayal gan, which, for practical purposes, means "Sitala's song," and *Olabibir gan* ("Olabibi's song") are, as their names imply, sung. A performance has the duality of an opera, complete with arias, duets, trios, choruses (none of these, unfortunately, harmonized), and recitative. There are also, as I mentioned before, interludes of Vaisnava *kirtans*, selected to match the mood in the story at the points in which they are introduced. The minimum musical accompaniment for any of these *gans* is the *khol* and *karatal*. The *khol* is a distinctively Bengali form of *mrdanga* with a pottery base, small and light enough to be suspended around the player's neck by a strap and danced with in delightful stylized steps. The *khol* is basically an accompaniment for Vaisnava *kirtan*, although it is played in almost any kind of religious music (and never with secular music). The *karatal* is a pair of small brass cymbals that also invariably accompany Vaisnava devotional singing and are used in other religious music, as well as in some secular music. Most of the *dals* also have a harmonium, about which the less said the better, from my point of view. Some use bamboo flutes as additional accompaniment and one group, which did a *yatra*-style performance of the myth, even used a cornet (which members of the group referred to as a "brass flute").

Almost all *sayal gan* performances are done in ordinary dress, with the lead singer — usually the man taking the part of *Sitala* — distinguished by a black yak-tail fly-whisk (*camar*) which he carries constantly. The fly-whisk is used to honor *Olabibi* during the afternoon offering of *puja* to her, and to honor *Sitala* during the *arati*, or display of lights before her image, in the early evening. The fly-whisk is thought to acquire some special power from these uses as well, perhaps, as from its being carried by someone representing *Sitala* herself. Thus, in groups that have Brahman members, the Brahman is also often the lead singer and may be the only one to handle the fly-whisk. However, in other *dals* the fly-whisk is constantly handled by Mahisyas and is even used by them to give blessings (by laying it on the back of the neck) to members of the audience.

One of the *dals* that I saw — the one that gave by far the most persuasive performance of the *Sitala-mangal* — used costumes and elaborate props, just as is done in the Bengali *yatra*. Members of the "orchestra" and "chorus" did not wear costumes, but all of the principal players — *Sitala, Jvarasur*, the ass, Nima the boatman and his wife, the Birat Raja and his chief queen Sudhesna, and Debdas Datta, the *sadhu* and physician, as well as a number of minor characters, were costumed. Some of the actors played several roles and the Fever Demon doubled as an instrumentalist.

In ordinary *sayal gan* performances there is usually a degree of dramatization that goes naturally with the fact that each singer enacts the role of only one character in each episode. Dramatization went much further than usual in the costumed performance, however, so that the major events in Nityananda's *Sitala-mangal* were communicated to the audience in an exceptionally persuasive manner. When the performance concluded, at about 2 a.m., many people, including almost all of the young married women with children in their arms, rushed forward to take dust from the feet of *Sitala*. The goddess in this case happened to be a young Mahisya man who had taken over the role from a Brahman, originally selected to play the part. This young Mahisya may have had the experience of having the dust reverentially taken from his feet on only a few previous occasions — perhaps by his younger sisters or by the young children of his elder sisters when they visited his house. When it happened after his performance of *Sitala*, he was evidently nonplussed at first; but he soon began to move among the audience, accepting reverence and allowing the dust to be taken from his feet, giving blessings (by the laying on of his fly-whisk), and accepting small coins as *daksina* (the fee of a Brahman). This event was, in my estimation, the clearest indication of the effectiveness of this oral and dramatic method of propagating the myth of *Sitala* that I saw. But the other forms of *sayal gan*, although less dramatically effective, are nonetheless persuasive reminders of what everyone already knows.

THE TRANSMISSION OF THE MYTH

The propagation of the myths of *Sitala* and *Olabibi* is done entirely through the oral and dramatic medium. Three media, however, are employed in transmitting the myths: Oral transmission, handwritten manuscripts, and printed material. Oral transmission takes place in the context of the *guru*-disciple relationship and in the somewhat more permissive version of this relationship that exists within the *sayal gan dal* between the leader (*malik*) of the group and its members. The leader has the role of artistic director for his company; he determines which portions of the myths are to be sung, which recited or enacted in dialogue, and which ommitted entirely.

Since each company attempts to make its performance distinctive and especially attractive, so that they will be employed more frequently, there is a good deal of variation in the presentation of those sections of the myth that are sung and great differences among *dals* in the language used in the songs.

Except for the fact that a manuscript may outlive a particular *guru*, in Bengal the transmission of myths by handwritten manuscripts is almost as private as the *guru*-disciple relationship itself. Manuscripts are generally transmitted either through the teacher-pupil lineage or through the family. Thus, discrepant versions of a myth, such as the *Olabibi gan*, may persist side by side over sustained periods of time, whether they are eighteenth century manuscripts, carefully written on country-made paper, or twentieth century ones, hastily written with blotting fountain pens in school notebooks.

A manuscript may have been used to teach hundreds of performers or may have lain untouched at a family shrine, receiving only ritual attention; in either case it exists apart from its author and so, while basically a private thing, it transmits its contents in an impersonal way. A greater degree of "dissociation" has occurred than would be the case in oral transmission.

Edward Sapir (1949: 566) speaks of varying degrees of "dissociation" between a symbol and "its original context". All of the words of any language, of course, are symbols in that they stand in a purely arbitrary relationship to the things, events, and relations to which they refer. Thus, it is sensible to say that the word, as a symbol, is dissociated from its referent in that the two bear no necessary or inherent relation to one another. There is an additional sense of "dissociation" between spoken and written words. The primary context of utilisation of linguistic symbols is in speech, that is, in direct communication between speaker and hearer; the ideal form of verbal communication is conversation, in which the responses of one person indicate to the other whether or not he is communicating what he intends. When words are written with the intention of communicating (as opposed to being written for mnemonic purposes), the dissociation is not only between symbol and referent and between the primary and secondary contexts of utilization, but also between the "encoder" and the "decoder" of the message. The reader is ordinarily deprived of the capacity to check the intention of the writer, although such a check is an inherent part of conversational use of language.

The Indian manuscript tradition is partially free from the communication problem inherent in writing. Insofar as the contents of a manuscript are taught by a preceptor to his disciples and, in recopying, are made more intelligible to succeeding generations of readers, the manuscript may be thought of as having a mnemonic function. Since manuscripts contain sacred knowledge, they are intended for specialist use and inevitably have esoteric aspects. In India, sacred knowledge is thought of as being powerful in itself; it should be made available only in limited degree to women and Sudras; the most esoteric aspects should be restricted to those who have been initiated by a particular *guru*.

Printing and publishing completes the dissociation between writer and reader. The marketing of printed books is absolutely contradictory to the idea of private knowledge, sacred or profane. The technology of printing implies the existence of a large enough literate population to constitute a "mass" market (although the definition of "mass" is obviously quite variable). The market, with the requirement that goods be displayed and attractively priced, and the anonymous relationship that exists between buyer and seller, means that esoterism cannot be preserved.[18] And the "mass" characteristic of the product means that it must be standardized.

18. A. K. Ramanujan (ms.) relates the story of the "most influential and probably the most thoroughgoing of the 19th and early 20th century

Standardization is not a common characteristic of Bengali manuscripts, however devoutly it may have been sought by writers and copyists. While the number of manuscripts of myths in Bengal can never have been very large, relative to the number of printed books that now exist, the lack of concord between any two of them supposedly relating the same material is so customary that scholars take it for granted. As I mentioned much earlier, the four versions of the *Sitala-mangal* that are known to Bengali literary scholars have little in common with one another than the goddess herself.[19] These were, of course, written by different men, at different times, and in different parts of Bengal. So long as they existed solely in manuscript and oral form only local tradition caused one to predominate over another.

Dimock and Ramanujan (1964) have examined a number of different texts of the *Manasa Mangal* and found that while they were written in quite different places at different times, they share a large common core. This is particularly true of the very popular episodes concerning the humbling of Cad Sadagar, the merchant prince, the killing of his youngest son Laksmindar, by one of *Manasa's* snakes, and his restoration to life through the devotion of his wife, Behula. In other words, there was a degree of standardization in the *Manasa* myths current in Bengal prior to their publication.

The printing of Nityananda's *Sitala-mangal*, changed the balance among the various *Sitalas*, even though several publishers issued ostensibly different popular editions. It seems possible that printing the myth in its various versions would have the potential diversifying as well as standardizing it. I have examined in a cursory way three cheap editions of the *Manasa Mangal* that were available in Bengali book stalls in 1968 and 1969; they appear to bear the same relationship to

---

Tamil scholars," Swaminatha Aiyar, who discovered in 1880 that for years he had been studying relatively late "second rate religious and grammatical texts" because sectarian strictures prevented his even coming to know of "the greatest of Tamil literary texts," the Sangam poetry. He was given, fortuitously, manuscripts of some of these to read. Thereafter, he devoted his life to findings, editing, and publishing Sangam poetry.

19. See note 7 above.

the originals as do *Reader's Digest* condensed books. While the author's language seems to be largely preserved, divergent *palas* have been eliminated so that the congruity among the various versions is increased. Thus, the effect of printing and publishing for a relatively large public has been the standardizing of Bengali mythology and, probably, the creating of a possible "orthodoxy" that may prevent further mythological development. Numerous copies of inexpensive *mangal* books, like museum reproductions of fossil animals, will remain to remind us of the past age of autonomy and creativity in the religion of rural Bengal.

REFERENCES CITED

Banerjea, Jitendra Nath
   1956 Development of Hindu Iconography. Calcutta, the University of Calcutta.
Basu Gopendrakrsna
   1969 *Bamlar Laukik Debata*. Second printing (First edition 1966). Calcutta, Ananda Publishers Private Limited.
Bhanj Deo, Prafulla Chandra
   1954 *Pisitasana*. Journal of the Asiatic Society, 3rd series 20: 1-5.
Bhattacarya, Asutos
   1952 The cult of the goddess of smallpox in West Bengal. The Quarterly Journal of the Mythic Society 43: 55-69.
   1964 *Bamla Mangalkavyer Itihasa*. Fourth edition (First edition 1950). Calcutta, A. Mukharji and Company.
Bhattacarya, Satyanarayana (editor)
   1958 *Kavi Krsnarama Daser Granthavali*. Calcutta, Calcutta University.
Bhattacarya, Tarapada
   1962 *Bangasahityer Itihasa (Pracin Parba)*. Calcutta, S. Gupta Brothers (Private) Ltd.
Buchanan Hamilton, Francis
   [1807- Account of the District or Zila of Dinajpur.
   1808] India Office Library, European Manuscripts, D.71.

Chakraberty, Chandra
   1923 An Interpretation of Ancient Hindu Medicine. Calcutta, Published by Ramchandra Chakraberty.
Cohen, Percy S.
   1969 Theories of myth. Man n.s. 4: 337-353.
Crooke, W.
   1968 The Popular Religion and Folk-Lore of Northern India. Third

reprint edition from the second edition of 1896. Delhi, Munshiram Manoharlal.

Das Gupta Tamonas Candra
1951 *Pracin Bangala Sahityer Itihasa*. Calcutta, Calcutta University.
Dimock, Edward C., Jr.
1963 The Thief of Love: Bengali Tales from Court and Village,. Chicago. The University of Chicago Press.
Dimock, Edward C., Jr., and A. K. Ramanujan
1964 The goddess of snakes in medieval Bengali literature. Part II. History of Religions 3: 300-322.
Dimock, Edward C., Jr., and Ronald B. Inden
1969 The City in pre-British Bengal, according to the *mangalakavyas*. In Urban Bengal, Richard L. Park, ed. East Lansing, Michigan State University Asian Studies Center Occasional Papers.

Ghos, Binay
1957 *Pascimbanger Samskrti*. Calcutta, Pustak Prakasak.
Goody, Jack and Ian Watt
1963 The consequences of literacy. Comparative Studies in Society and History 5: 304-345.

Hein, Norvin
1958 The *Ram Lila*. In Singer 1958: 279-304.
Hora, Sunder Lal
1933 Worship of the deities Ola, Jhola, and Bon Bibi in Lower Bengal. Journal of the Asiatic Society of Bengal, n.s. 29: 1-4.

Inden, Ronald
1967 The Hindu chiefdom in middle Bengali literature. In Bengal: Literature and History, Edward C. Dimock, Jr., ed. East Lansing, Michigan State University Asian Studies Center Occasional Papers.

Marriott, McKim
1959 Changing channels of cultural transmission in Indian civilization. In Intermediate Societies, Social Mobility, and communication. Proceedings of the 1959 Annual Spring Meeting of the American Ethnological Society. Seattle, University of Washington.
McCormack, William
1958 The forms of communication in Virasaiva religion. In Singer 1958: 325-335.
Mukhopadhyaya Bhaktibhusana, Gopaldasa (compiler)
1965 *Stavakavacamala*. Revised by Kumaranatha Sudhakara. Third edition. Calcutta, Published by Bijanabasini Devi.

Nityananda [Cakravarti] ("dvija Nityananda")

1931 Brhat Sitala Mangal ba Sitalar Jagarana Pala. Calcutta, Tarachand Das and Sons.

Raghavan, V.
1958 Methods of popular religious instruction in South India. In Singer 1958: 336-344.

Ramanujan, A. K.
ms. Language and 'modernization': the Tamil example.

Sapir, Edward
1949 Selected Writings of Edward Sapir in Language, Culture, and Personality, D. G. Mandelbaum, ed. Berkeley, University of California Press.

Sen, Dinesh Chandra
1954 History of Bengali Language and Literature. Second edition. Calcutta, The University of Calcutta.

Sen, Sukumar
1960 History of Bengali Literature, New Delhi, Sahitya Akademi.

Sengupta, J. C., and Sanat Kumar Bose (editors)
1962 West Bengal District Records. New series. Midnapore. Letters Received, 1777-1800. [Calcutta, Government of West Bengal.]

Singer, Milton (editor)
1958 Traditional India: Structure and Change. [A special issue of the] Journal of American Folklore 71 (no. 281).

Singer, Milton
1958 The great tradition in a metropolitan center: Madras. In Singer 1958:347-388.

Whitehead, Henry
1921 The Village Gods of South India. Second Edition. Calcutta, Association Press.

11

A KERALA VILLAGE TEMPLE FESTIVAL: RITUAL AND FOLK ART FORMS AS COMMUNICATORS OF TRADITIONAL CULTURE

CLIFFORD R. JONES

In Kerala the temples are still the principal repositories of the continuity of traditional Hindu art as it has been preserved in the past and continues in the present. The range of temple art forms and their particular expression and articulation in Kerala are regional traditions stemming from ancient Tamil roots overlaid and integrated with Sanskrit culture. These traditions seem to have reached their widest development in the late medieval period with the emergence of Malayalam as a language of literature. In Kerala the temple-centered arts of architecture, sculpture, painting, recitation, music, dance and drama, integrated with religious ritual, embody and express many of the great all-India themes and concepts found in the epic literature and mythology of the *puranas*. The specific articulation of these themes and concepts is strongly governed by local traditions of *sastra*, *tantra*, or *agama*-based schools of practice.

The oldest surviving form of presenting Sanskrit drama in India, called *Kutiyattam*, is one of these several temple-centered arts. Among other performing arts are the fairly well-known *Kathakali* dance-drama and lesser-known dramatic forms such as *Krsnattankali* dance-drama, *Cakyar Kuttu*, *Ottan Tullal*, *Pathakam*, etc. All these dramatic forms in greater or lesser degree are a living continuity with literature and art as traditionally performed. They range from the most didactic philosophical verities to interpolations of often bawdy satire for the sheer pleasure of entertainment. The familiar shapes and images, color patterns and embellishments of these dramatic forms are the visual carriers of an important corpus of abstract and symbolic ideas. On specific occasions each of these temple drama forms finds a place within a temple festival celebration.

Still less-known are the rituals and dramatic forms employed by the service and agriculturist "castes" of Kerala society in their festival celebrations. For instance, during the annual festival of *Puram Vela*,[1] at which time the goddess Bhagavati is worshipped, the focus is shifted from the Sanskritic patterns of Brahmanical orthodoxy of the upper castes to a dominance of folk ritual and expression of perhaps an earlier pre-Aryan ancestry. Here the mass of participants are from the groups below Sudras, with the exception of a few key priests and specialists. The costumed dances, dramatic mimes and ritual processions which take place at these festivals are virtually unknown outside of Kerala.

Within the basic pattern of events in the celebration of the *Puram Vela* festival for Bhagavati are two unique ritual performances, *Tolpava Kuttu*, found only in Central Kerala, and *Bhagavati Pattu*. Both require specialists from castes above the service castes and below the orthodox ranks of the Nambutiris. One of these specialists is the *tantri*[2] or priest who performs *puja* for the special ceremony called *Bhagavati Pattu*. This last also requires the services of two members of the *Kuruppu* community, two Nayar drummers, and a Nayar *veliccappatu* priest who is permanently in service to the particular Bhagavati *Kavu* (shrine). The services of Nayar and *Cetti* Puluvar puppeteers are needed for *Tolpava Kuttu*, the ceremonial presentation of the shadow puppet drama of the *Ramayana*. Other specialists are the professionally trained musicians, Sudras, Ambalavasis, and occasionally Nambutiris,

---

1. Puram is the name of an asterism. Gundert defines Puravela as "the Saturnalia of Malabar, a feast in Kumbha (end of March in memory of Kama's death... ." H. Gundert, *A Malayalam and English Dictionary*, Kottayam: Sahitya Pravarthaka C. S. Ltd., 2nd ed., 1962, p. 642.

2. The *tantri* or priest referred to is, as is usual in a Bhagavati *kavu*, an Embrantiri or Tulu Brahmana immigrant ranked traditionally below the subdivisions of Nambutiris and above Pattar Brahmanas from Tamil Nadu.

who form the temple orchestra, an historically later addition to the festival.

This paper deals principally with the *Puram Vela* in honour of Kozhimambarambu Bhagavati in the village of Cheruthuruthi. It provides limited description of the pattern and form of the festival including identification of participating castes and specialists and notes on costumes and ceremonial instruments. A full range of potential symbols from sympathetic magic to social and political history is implicit in the present description. A brief discussion of the communication of socio-religious, literary, and artistic concepts and ideas is presented in the concluding section.

Only one small facet of the larger complex of related temple festivals in Central Kerala can be examined here. We are calling attention to a particularly rich area of traditional culture still unstudied.

Background

In the geographic area of Central Kerala under examination (Talappilli Taluk in Trichur District of old Cochin State and Ottappalam Taluk of Palghat District of old South Malabar), there is a traditional ranked system of interrelationships called *tattakam* among shrines and temples belonging to the *manas*, *taras*, and *ceris* (traditionally the village areas of Nambutiri Brahmanas, Nayar-Sudras, and lower ranked communities, respectively). The *tattakam* or *mandalam* is a "circle" of interrelating ranked shrines subordinate to a main shrine or temple.[3]

The traditions connected with these temples and the *sthala purana* or "old tale of the place" of each individual local shrine indicate historical or quasi-historical political relation-

---

3. A traditional ranked pattern of interrelationship in similar form is known to have existed also among a number of the important Brahmanical temples formerly associated with the royal houses of Kerala. For example, the legendary eighteen *tali* temples of the Trichur area are believed to have been associated historically with the second Cera dynasty, circa 8th century A.D. Whether this relationship followed the pattern of political or religious influence, or cut across them, is not yet known.

ships between areas in the *tattakam*, and ultimately seem to determine the particular geographic patterns of the interrelated shrines. The *tattakam* we shall examine briefly is composed of three smaller groups of interrelated shrines participating in the *Puram Vela* of the Bhagavati shrine at the village of Cheruthuruthi. There are two similar adjacent independent *tattakams*, both about fifteen miles distant. One of these culminates at *Ariyyan Kavu* which is located in Ottappalam Taluk of Palghat District. The other, in Talappilli Taluk of Trichur District, culminates in the *Tritala Candi Kavu*. These two *tattakams* remain to be investigated. There are some fifteen such complexes in Eastern Trichur District and Palghat District, all sharing very similar features and significantly connected by the fact that the *Ramayana* shadow puppet drama is performed in all of them by a group of Tamil Cetti Puluvar families. Beyond this group of Bhagavati shrines, the performance of the *Ramayana* shadow puppet drama is found nowhere else in Kerala or Tamil Nadu. Our examination deals with only a small part of this special larger network of Bhagavati shrines in Eastern Central Kerala.

The village of Cheruthuruthi is located in Talappilli Taluk of Trichur District, Central Kerala State, on the west bank of the Bharatapuzha River and one mile west of the railway junction of Shoranur. The Bharatapuzha River separates Shoranur in Palghat District from Cheruthuruthi in Trichur District. Here each year in the Malayalam month of *Kumbham* (February-March) the festival called *Puram Vela* is celebrated in honour of Kozhimambarambu Bhagavati.

In Trichur District, the yearly worship of Bhagavati in the local village shrines is culminated by the annual pilgrimage to the Kodungalur Kurumba Bhagavati temple. The pilgrimage takes place at the time of the *Bharani Naksatram* festival in the month of *Minam* (March-April). There appears to be a related pattern among other Bhagavati shrines in Central Kerala in that almost all of them hold their local festival before this annual pilgrimage.

The Kodungalur festival is considered to be the most important in Kerala. The temple is located in the immediate vicinity of the ancient capital of the Cera kings, which was centered around the present-day town of Kodungahur in Cranganore Taluk, Trichur District. Kodungalur is near the sea, about thirty-five miles to the southwest of Cheruthuruthi. The pilgrims come from as far away as Cannanore District in the north and Alleppey District in the south. The largest groups participating are from the social strata below Nayars.

It seems to be clear that the cult of the goddess, both as a war goddess and a disease protectress, has been established in this area of Kerala and among a large part of Kerala society since quite ancient times. The oldest historical or literary references are in early Tamil literature, about 2nd to 5th century A.D. It is believed that there may be a connection between the Kodungalur Bhagavati and the ancient Tamil war goddess Kottavai (Dravidian Durga) who is mentioned in old Tamil literature. The local importance of the Kodungular temple is emphasized by a legend connecting it with the story of the deified Kannaki, the chaste and long-suffering heroine of the *Cilappatikaram*. It is believed that the temple at Kodungular was founded by the Cera Emperor Cengkuttuvan, the legendary hero-king celebrated in the Tamil epic.[4] Referring to the ancient capital of the Ceras, it is said that, "To the Greeks and Romans it was known as 'Muziris' from the ancient temple whose Goddess was called 'Masuri Devata' on account of her power to ward off small-pox...".[5] Masuri Devata may be a confusion with Vasurimala, a name of the local smallpox goddess. A pilgrimage to this temple during the festival period is considered to be a potential deterrent to small-pox, cholera, and other infectious diseases.

The worship of a mother goddess presiding over disease, particularly small-pox and cholera, is a fairly prevalent practice throughout the south. The village Ammans of Tamil Nadu are almost invariably disease goddesses. Whitehead, speaking of Tamil Nadu and its village cults, quotes from an article by F. J. Richards, I.C.S.: "The cholera goddess is popu-

---

4. A. Sreedhara Menon, *Kerala District Gazetteers — Trichur,* Trivandrum: Government of Kerala Press, 1962, pp. 89-92. Also see V. T. Induchudan, *The Secret Chamber,* Cochin: Cochin Devasvom Board Press, 1969.
5. Menon, op. cit., p. 612.

larly believed to be the mother of the washerman. He is
therefore chosen to officiate as the *pujari*, as the son alone can
hope to succeed in propitiating such a fierce divinity."[6]

In Kerala the Vannam and Velan castes, two subdivisions
of the washerman castes, trace their creation to the goddess
Parvati, another form of Bhagavati.[7] Although the Vannan
and Velan groups alone maintain a special creation myth relating to the goddess, the other castes participating in the Bhagavati festival at Cheruthuruthi all hold Bhagavati to be their
patron goddess or ancestral deity. Bhagavati is not worshipped exclusively by the lower castes in Kerala, but is revered
by all Hindu communities, particularly the Nayars, for whom
she is the *kalari devata*, or goddess of the military gymnasium
that is, the war goddess and protectress.

At this point a brief description of the goddess as Bhagavati or Kali is in order. In Kerala the goddess is conceived
as a fearsome manifestation, warlike, terrible, black or red,
with protruding canine tusks and wild flying hair, covered
with all manner of ornamentation, four- or eight-armed, and
carrying sword, trident, shield, the severed head of the demon
Dharika, serpent, bell, skull cup and pestle, etc. This visual
conception varies in different parts of the country and with
the wealth of the temple. Some images or paintings are relatively simple while others are richly ornamented, demonstrating
a concept of hieratic iconography and symbolism universally
acknowledged in Kerala. This tradition stems from the *Tantrasamuccaya*, a *tantra silpa* text of the 15th century, composed in Central Kerala.

---

6. Rev. Henry Whitehead, *The Village Gods of South India*, Calcutta:
Associated Press, 1921, p. 38. Another myth gives the Tamil washerman as a descendant of the demon-hero Virabhadra (an emanation of
Siva) who was ordered by Siva to wash the clothes of all men as an
expiation of the sin of putting so many people to death at the destruction of Daksa's *yaga*. This *yaga* was the ritual fire sacrifice or *homam*
of Daksa into which Sati, daughter of Daksa and wife of Siva, threw
herself, committing suicide. The fire sacrifice was destroyed by the will
of Siva in the form of Virabhadra and Bhadrakali, during the course
of which many people were killed, including Brahmanas.

7. L. K. Anantha Krishna Iyer, *The Cochin Tribes and Castes*, Madras
Higginbotham and Company, 1912, Vol. I, p. 156.

At the Kodungalur festival rice, salt, chillis, betel leaves and areca nuts, turmeric powder, and pepper form part of the traditional offerings. A general atmosphere of permissiveness, festival drinking, carrying phalli in procession, and the recitation of a series of erotic and obscene songs are distinguishing features of the festival at Kodungalur. These are continued into the present-day ritual celebrations, suggesting the secondary aspect of Bhagavati as a fertility goddess who protects, destroys and quickens the seed of procreation.

The sacrifice of live chickens for the propitiation of the goddess, once held in the outer boundary of the shrine, has been altered. Blood sacrifice was discontinued in 1954 in pursuance of the Travancore-Cochin Act of 1953, The Birds Sacrifices Prohibition Act. Instead, as a symbolic act, the piligrims let a cock fly in front of the stone altar near the shrine,[8] or throw packets of turmeric and spices as well as coconuts and short sticks over the walls into the inner court of the shrine.

The Kodungalur Bharani is the single most important focal point of the tradition of Bhagavati worship in Kerala. The festival at Kodungalur has quite a distinct expression and ritual from the Bhagavati festival at Cheruthuruthi. Further studies may bring into better focus these important segments of Kerala religious life in the rural folk context.

The Daytime Ceremony

The Bhagavati shrine of Kozhimambarambu is situated on the western boundary of the village of Cheruthurithi. It stands in an open field in the center of a gently sloping bluff surrounded by cultivated paddy. Like many temples and old manor houses in Kerala, it is built on a high place and for a good part of the year it is isolated, standing like an island in the midst of a sea of green paddy fields. It has the usual characteristics of Kerala's rural architecture, essentially unpretentious and simple in form, but immediately recognizable as a definite style. Small and unassuming, the shrine is about forty by forty feet in area, closely walled in. A gigantic *alu* (pipal) tree some fifty feet high dwarfs the low white plaster

---

8. Menon, op. cit., p. 613.

and wood structure roofed in terracotta tiles. From a distance it appears to be the most unimportant of shrines.

The last rice crop had been harvested in the month of *Makaram* (January-February), and the flooded fields had dried in the burning sun. At the time of the *Puram Vela* festival in the month of *Kumbham*, these same fields are filled with people. Near the shrine a street of shops and stalls had sprung up overnight. In anticipation of the crowds, three wooden country ferris-wheels and a small traveling circus had established themselves. The people had come from the surrounding countryside, many of them on foot, bringing mats and bedding and in many cases cooking vessels, with the simple intent of staying the length of the festival out in the open fields.

The festival day marking the end of the cycle of celebrated days was the most impressive. The procession was divided into three separate parties which began at different geographic points, each about one to three miles from the temple. Each of the three places was a sacred spot, a temple shrine or sacred tree. One of the parties originated at Nadumpura to the north-west, and another at Puducheri to the north. These two segments, each having its own subdivisions, formed part of the total *tattakam* performing in the festival.

The eastern line of the procession representing the village of Cheruthuruthi began at an old *alu* tree about fifty or sixty feet high and about five feet in diameter at the base. The tree is surrounded by a raised *altara* of masonry and tamped earth; at the four cardinal points of the compass, monolithic stone posts are placed. These are about two and a half feet high with a shallow hollowed-out surface at the top, the four dressed sides aligned with the cardinal directions. On special occasions the shallow hollow is filled with oil and becomes a lamp; the four lamps are lighted and *puja* is performed. Often older people of the vicinity stop at this tree for morning prayers on their way back from early bathing in the adjacent Bharatapuzha River where there is a small temple to Siva.

A *puja* had just been completed at the base of the tree. Onto the raised *altara*, now decorated with *kuruttola* (palm fringe) tied like a garland around the trunk of the tree, a fully caparisoned tusker was led. A man riding on the elephant's back helped to lift up a *kolam tatambu*, or ikon, of Siva. This ikon he held in place as if it were a shield, resting on the elephant's neck. The elephant, a magnificent animal about ten feet high at the shoulder, was led clockwise, circummambulating the tree once, then led some hundred yards through the fields to the main road of the village approaching the temple of Bhagavati from the Bharatapuzha River. Here the ikon was met by two more elephants similarly decorated. They were each mounted at this point by two more men, the first of which held a large pair of circular *alavattam*, fans of peacock feathers. The round centres of the *alavattam* were decorated with white *mayil pili* (peacock feather quills) and with red, green and gold metallic papers in an intricate and very striking geometric design; the circumference was bordered with peacock feather tips. The second man carried a pair of snow white *camaram* or whisks made of yak fur with silver pommels. The rider holding the red felt-covered "shield" of the ikon with its gold bas-relief of the god's image surrounded with courses of decorative gold bosses, now held a silver-fringed satin umbrella aloft as well, adding still more paraphernalia.

In front of the three elephants, ranged row on row was the famous Kerala *pancavadyam* or temple orchestra composed of four *ilattalam* (bronze cymbals); one *itekka* (a tunable double-headed drum suspended by a sling over the shoulder and resting on the left hip, played with a delicate curved stick of red sandalwood); four *maddalam* (a heavy double-headed, horizontal drum played with the hands); four *timila* (a slim vertical drum with slightly concave sides, played on the left hip); four *kombu* (the huge curving bronze horn, not unlike the medieval French hunting horn); plus one man with *samkhu* or conch shell — a total of eighteen men. All were upper-caste professional musicians.

Gradually the procession moved forward to the slow, heavily measured beat of the first rhythmic pattern set by the musicians. The sounding of all the percussion instruments simultaneously in a slow, dirge-like tempo, created a deep booming pulse of drums with higher metallic overtones and harmonics, topped by the shimmer of the heavy bell-metal cymbals. The fringed brilliant red and gold forehead ornamentation of the elephants, above that the ikon and blazing cerise satin umbrella, with its pendant silver fringes swaying to the ponderous movement of the huge white-tusked animals, bombarded the eye with glittering display. This opulence was set into high relief by the simple costume of the elephant drivers, musicians, and villagers who were, as is the old Malayali custom, dressed almost exclusively in white cotton, grouped against the gleaming white tusks and dark shadowy shapes of the mounted elephants. The whole impression of this spectacle was dignified and powerful. The blinding sunlight sparkled on the green masses of arching coconut palms against a brilliant cloudless sky. Waves of excited expectation rippled through the throngs on either side, and as the procession moved forward, one could physically feel the pulse of growing vitality as the rhythm took form and began to build slowly, leisurely, to carry the procession to its final destination.

The line of the procession moved at a slow, even, steady gait, stopping only at intervals of about 500 feet for orchestral interludes of increasingly complex drumming, doubling and redoubling upon itself, building to bursting crescendos and resolving again into one slow pulsing rhythm, then moving on as the drums subsided into a simple marking beat. As we approached the open fields surrounding the little raised area of the temple ground, we could at last see the two other groups of caparisoned elephants coming into view, far across the field. The last several hundred yards around the temple, being free of trees and cottages, gave a sweeping view of whiteclad villagers by the thousands thronging the area, and towering above them the three swaying lines of elephants converging on the shrine. A little to one side of the direct line of the entrance to the inner shrine was the assembly point for the gathering processions of elephants and musicians.

Various local groups of the Vannan caste had already arrived in advance of the elephant processions. These groups contributed their own special votive arts of *bhutam* and *tira*, simple but vigorous rhythmic dances. Wearing bells at their waists and *cilambu*[9] on their ankles, turning, stamping, and wheeling in repeated simple choreographic patterns, the Vannan devotees held their ground immediately before the temple entrance.

At the main road about 200 yards away were three Paraya-Ceruma *veliccappatus*, each representing the goddess Bhagavati, dressed in traditional regalia with false bronze breasts and tusks and a bizarre makeup of intense color and primitive design. They stood on palanquins, ready to make their entrance, accompanied by their own drummers. Behind them, in a separate group, also on palanquins carried by Pulaya-Cerumas, were life sized effigies of horses *(kutira)* and bullocks *(kala)* of bamboo covered in straw-stuffed cloth and paper, decorated in red, white and black with bits of silver and gold, their straw manes and tails constantly blowing in the wind. The better of these animal effigies had extremely well-carved and painted, life-sized, wooden heads, the work of the local *Asari* or carpenter-woodcarver. The Paraya-Ceruma palanquin bearers (four for each Bhagavati, dressed in red, black and white), poised themselves for a dizzy, jostling run down the slight incline to the area immediately to the side of the shrine, in front of the *kuttumatam* or shadow puppet theatre. Their entrance was heralded by increased drumming and shouting as the bearers pranced about, dipping up and down. The Pulaya-Ceruma palanquin bearers of the horse and bullock animal effigies imitated even more realistically the prancing of animals, rearing up, alternately retreating and rushing forward.

They all at last assembled in their respective groups to the left of the shrine. The palanquins were set down and, as the drums continued and intensified their steady rhythm, the three Paraya-Ceruma Bhagavatis remained in their "chariots," their bodies agitated and trembling, with their swords raised

---

9. A *cilambu* is a kind of hollow anklet made of bronze and filled with metal shot to make it jingle. It is oval in shape, worn below the ankle bone and attached by a string loop to the first or second toe. *Cilambu* are commonly worn by *veliccappatus* and by devotees of Bhagavati and Ayyappan, both in Kerala and on the East Coast, when engaged in a religious festival or ceremony. A third *cilambu* is also often held in the left hand.

up and shaking. In the left hand they held a *cilambu* with which they kept up a steady whirring rhythm. Their eyes staring in concentration, for hours they trembled until finally they appeared to be genuinely self-hypnotized; then they descended from their chariots, and paced wildly up and down, uttering half audible oracles. The drummers for the dancers and the "three Bhagavatis" were quite separate ensembles from the more elaborate higher-caste percussion orchestra in front of the elephants.

Assembled in the forecourt beyond the outer walls facing the shrine, the elephants formed a natural backdrop for the caste orchestra with its changing orders of ranks for *pancavadyam, melam,* and *panti melam* — orchestral compositions for percussion and wind instruments, traditionally a part of Kerala temple ceremony. The three Paraya-Ceruma Bhagavatis, with their palanquins and drummers, were a little to the right and forward, facing the shrine, but near the *Kuttumatam*. In front of the shrine before the elephants and their orchestra, three masked Vannan dancers wheeled about like swooping birds caressing the earth, accompanied by a caste member playing the *para*, a small double-headed drum played with a slender stick.

Six other figures (belonging to the Velan caste) with white- and black-smeared faces stamped and wheeled about nearby. Their heads were surmounted by huge semicircular teak headdresses ornamented with handsomely carved sacred figures of Gajalaksmi and bordered with a horizontal arc of peacock feathers three feet high. The heavy towering wooden headdress was balanced on the head by two long cloth tassels, one on each side of the arc, held firmly in each hand by the devotee-dancer as he performed his twisting, dipping, advancing, retreating patterns. All the while the *cilambu* on his ankles and large bronze bells at his waist set off a constant whirring clangor. Each of the accompanying percussion orchestras was an independent unit playing its own rhythms; the total conflicting percussive effect was staggering.

The noon *puja* had been performed in the sanctum of the shrine by the Embrantiri priest. From the entrance of the shrine three Nayar *vel'ccappatus* brought forward *prasadam* (sanctified offering) in the form of brilliant red *kumkumam* powder on large brass trays. These they held in the left hand; like the three *"devis"* they each held an ancient ritual sword in the right hand. One sword was curved at the top like a sickle, a second had a *trisulam*-tipped blade, and the third an undulating flame-like shape. All three were of equal length, broad and heavy with worked brass hilts and embellished with tiny bronze cobras and pendant bells. The ceremonial swords were made by the master *Karuvan* or blacksmith of the nearby hamlet of Vazhalikavu. These Nayar priests, who normally wear their hair long in the old Kerala fashion, knotted on the left side or at the back of the head, now unbound their hair which fell to their waists. They were ceremonially dressed in blood red waistcloths over their usual white. Red is the symbolic color of the goddess. They wore heavy bronze belts of bells about their waists and *cilambu* on each ankle. The belts of bells and *cilambu* were the craftsmanship of the Musari or bronze caster community. One of the Nayar priests, an old and very dignified man, had striking long white hair; another had black shining hair whipping about his waist. The villagers pressed forward and placed offerings of coins on the trays; they smudged some *kumkumam* on their foreheads, while the priests laid the flat of the sword on their heads in token of the goddess's blessing.

All the while the drumming, never once stopping, continued to build in intensity and complexity. Groups of drummers performed independent of each other, creating a layered sound effect. Waves of rhythm burst out in swelling crescendos. In the ensemble of upper-caste professional musicians, at regular intervals the *kombu* players began building a dazzling rhythmic pattern layer upon layer up the scale, with trumpets blazing above shimmering bronze cymbals and relentless drums. At the very peak of the progression the effect was agonizingly sustained, with the sound repeating over and over in a wildly tossing frenetic exultation, until the *alavattam* and *camaram* bearers suddenly stood up on the elephants' backs. The *camaram* bearers in unison twirled and swung the huge white plumes back and forth in arcs, making visual the pulse of the rhythm. Suddenly the rhythm fell back, descending to a murmur of drumming. This pattern was meticulously repeated at about twenty-minute intervals, building to sustained crescendos, falling back, building another rhythmic structure, again, and again, for several hours, forming a brilliant ;*tour de force* in the continuous fabric of ceremonial drumming.

The emotional intensity steadily mounted as the day grew hotter. There seemed to be, somewhere not far beneath the surface, a thread of hysteria in the concentrated energy of the ritual performance. The marathon-like celebration of the festival was the means by which the goddess' devotees gave visual and audial expression of homage.

The Evening Ceremony

The evening ceremony began with a repetition of the pattern of the daytime festival procession from the *alu* tree. After the elephants had been bathed and decorated, the procession formed together in the same way and proceeded through the village street toward the shrine. The total effect by night was far more stimulating. For lighting, instead of the now common Petromax gasoline lamp with its blinding white light, traditional *kol vilakku* (hand-held lamps with oil and wick) were carried in front of each elephant. The scene was also lit with torches and from time to time with brilliant cerise flares (of the kind used in the United States to mark an accident or repairs on the highway). Their use to light the ornately caparisoned elephants and massed drummers was brilliantly theatrical. The same processional pattern as earlier was observed, using pauses for rhythmic orchestral effects, and a slow, solemn, marked tempo; the drums kept a simple rhythm.

When they reached the precincts of the shrine, the elephants and musicians were arranged in the same pattern as during the day. In addition, portable branched lamps five feet high, each with five large wicks, were stuck in the ground in a row. These were set between the elephants and the drummers in a straight line, the elephants facing the shrine and the musicians and drummers facing the elephants. Everything was bathed in a warm flickering light. The vigorous bustling

A Kerala Village Temple Festival

vesams or "characterization" of the Vannans, Velans, and Cerumas of the daylight festival did not participate in the evening ceremony.

Presently a bell was rung in the shrine and a Nayar *veliccappatu* stepped forward to receive a bronze plate with a flaming wick from the *tantri*. The *veliccappatu* circumambulated the shrine and then the tree, followed by two other *veliccappatus*. They approached an old foundation stone facing the *kuttumatam* (the theater for the shadow puppet drama), raised their swords, shaking them on high, and cried out long and clear, "Hi -i - a-a-a-a-a," the last syllable dying away like a suppliant's wail.

From the little theater the senior *Puluvar* puppeteer came forward and received the sacred flame. With the flame he lighted a bunch of lamp wicks prepared for the occasion and made a clockwise circle with the wicks in the air on a vertical plane, invoking the *sakti* of the goddess. He then turned and walked swiftly back to the theater and entered to the beat of a *para* drum. He quickly dropped a lighted wick into each of the coconut-shell lamps behind the white cloth screen stretched taut across the theater front; behind this white cloth the shadows of the leather puppets would soon appear. From stage right to left, one after the other of the lamps was lighted. There were some thirty wicks in all, causing an even rising glow behind the curtain. A long-chanted introduction then began with the invocation of the *gurus* and gods. The prolonged anticipation was sustained as one by one each of the characters appeared in the prelude; finally the drama of the *Ramayana* began to unfold. The performance each evening ended only in the early hours of dawn.

Puluvar is a title meaning "scholar" among local Tamil Cettis. They are often hereditary puppeteers. The *Puluvars* concerned with the Cheruthuruthi festival come from nearby villages in Palghat District which borders Tamil Nadu. They claim to have immigrated from Madurai in "ancient times." The *Puluvars* speak Tamil in their homes as well as Malayalam in their day to day business. The text of the *Ramayana* used by them for *Tolpava Kuttu* (literally, "leather puppet play") is the *Kamba Ramayana* (circa 10th century) written in old Tamil. To the text have been added many Malayalam interpolations and Sanskrit *slokas* as well as passages of free improvization including a good deal of racy humor.

It is a custom in Palghat and Eastern Trichur Districts to have shadow puppet performances of the *Ramayana* story performed in this season (*Kumbham* and *Minam*) at Bhagavati shrines. The play is given in a permanent brick and plaster or temporary shed-like theater, made according to specific dimensions, which always faces the goddess. In former times it was a rule at festivals that the play be performed for a cycle of twenty-one nights, ending on the last night with the coronation of Rama. In the present time, however, the play is reduced to a shorter series, usually of five days.[10] The full cycle of twenty-one days is still maintained at Ariyyan Kavu. There are some fifteen Bhagavati *kavus* in Palghat and Trichur Districts served by these *Puluvar* families, augmented in each place by local Nayar Kavis who assist in the performances, chanting, speaking, and manipulating the puppets.

The association of the *Ramayana* shadow play with Bhagavati shrines is of interest. According to myth, the god Paramesvara instituted the *Ramayana* shadow play for the enjoyment of Bhadrakali (another name for Bhagavati) who had missed seeing the battle of Lanka, being engaged elsewhere at the time, destroying the demon Dharika. Aside from the mythical origin, Kamba, the author of the Tamil version of the *Ramayana*, was an Uvacchan by caste, Uvacchans being *arccakas* or assisting priests in Kali temples in Tamil Nadu.[11]

The puppets are specially made by master Asari carpenters who are woodcarvers and work in ivory as well. The leather used is traditionally untanned black deer skin, but buffalo hide is also used. The designs are elaborately pierced with

---

10. M. D. Raghavan, *Folk Plays and Dances of Kerala,* Trichur: Rama Varma Archaeological Society, 1947, pp. 37-42. Also, K. P. Narayana Pisharoti, *Kalalokam,* Trichur: The Mangalodayam (Private) Ltd., 1960, pp. 35-36 (Malayalam).

11. K. A. Nilakanta Sastri, *The Cholas,* Madras: University of Madras, 1955, p. 671.

special tools in decorative style. Although they are painted and articulated, they present only moving opaque shadows. They can be of very fine quality. The finest and largest set of over one hundred and fifty pieces is owned by the Kavalappara palace family. Some families of *Puluvars* and a few temples possess their own sets; otherwise they are rented for a performance.

Bhagavati Pattu

Besides the *Ramayana* shadow puppet play, *Bhagavati Pattu* is the other important ritual art form of dramatic type associated with the *Puram Vela* festival. The ritual is repeated on successive nights immediately before the festival proper begins. It is a form of votive offering made by individuals or groups of devotees. The drawing of an elaborate picture of the goddess Bhagavati upon the floor of a hall adjacent to the shrine is the central motif of the ritual. The ceremony requires the services of several specialists: an Embrantiri Brahmana priest, a Nayar *Veliccappatu*, two Nayar drummers, and two Kuruppu artist-singers belonging to a special service caste.

The elaborate picture of the goddess must be drawn by the Kuruppu artists in five colored powders according to a highly prescribed pattern; it takes about four hours to complete. When it is finished the Embrantiri priest performs a *puja* according to tantric formula. Then the Kuruppu artists seat themselves at the left side of the drawing and, to the accompaniment of a drone instrument, they recount in song the myth of the goddess Bhagavati from her creation to the dramatic moment of her destruction of the evil demon Dharika.[12] Not only does this ceremony enact the story of the goddess through the art of drawing and a sung text, it is further embellished with a choreographed ritual danced by the Nayar Shaman priest. In the course of the ritual dance the Nayar priest becomes possessed by the goddess and speaks

---

12. The size of the drawing in colored powder averages about ten by eleven feet in area. There are eighteen forms of deity represented in the repertoire of the ritual artists, each with a descriptive sung text accompanying it.

oracles to the patrons of the ceremony. These oracles express the pleasure or displeasure of the goddess; if she is pleased it is of course auspicious. On those rare occasions when she is not, the content of the oracle will give the reasons. It may be that the patron has slighted some deity or person; more often it is simply because the ceremony was not elaborate enough or properly provided for.

At the end of the ceremony the drawing in powders is swept up; the "corpus of the image" in the powder, mixed with consecrated unhusked rice, is then thrown in a shower upon each of the devotees. *Prasadam* is given to all in the form of red *kumkumam* powder, scented ash, sandal paste, sweets, and flowers sanctified as offerings to the goddess. The significance of the powder thrown upon the devotees is clear. It is the protection of the goddess against disease extended in the form of a symbolic contact or communion.

Levels of Communication

The ritual observance of religious obligations in the form of offerings, supplications, prayers, and communion with a protective, generative deity is a source of spiritual and psychological satisfaction to the villagers. The traditional myths and literature are not only integrated with the specific magico-religious rituals of the priests, but are dramatized as if they were taking place within the contemporary cultural landscape of Kerala. With familiar pictorial representations in brilliant colors and in shadow images stimulating to the subconscious, the dramatic rituals of epic heroes, demons, and divine intervention are incorporated into their annual cycle. The timeless day-to-day hopes, fears, and desires of the people take shape again and again in symbolic forms.

Traditional religious ideals are acted out and participated in by the villagers, each in his specified role, now actor, now audience. The impressions of the total visual experience of the festival, apart from its specific content, communicate in abstract ways the continuity of local culture. This communication is non-specific, non-literal. The aesthetic enjoyment of the excellence of the whole artistic display, of the formal dignity and style of execution of the various stages and segments of the total festival, culminating in the seemingly mundane orgasm of fireworks, enhances the villager's feeling of pride and accomplishment and tends to reinforce his feeling of wellbeing in his immediate society. The total environment of this audio-visual experience has a commmunication impact which can only be suggested here within the limitations of verbal description.

The Festival Organization and Change

Formerly the *Puram Vela* festivals were organized by the participating caste groups themselves, providing their own costumes and properties for the procession and subsequent ceremony, much as they do now. They traditionally raised funds to support this by going from house to house in the proper season before the festival, drumming and dancing, the occasion of which was, and in many cases still is, believed to bring "good luck." For this traditional service they were paid in kind; an additional few annas were sometimes given. Usually the houses visited were those with which a traditional *jajmani* relationship was established, or those for which some occasional service had been performed.

Some fifty years ago, there were no stately elephants connected with the festival. These and the addition of the Embrantiri priest and of paid upper-caste musicians are innovations of the modern period of further "Sanskritization." They are elements borrowed from or in imitation of larger Brahmanical Hindu temple festivals in more urban areas. In this respect there is an element of competition among the related three major processions as to which produces the best elephants and trappings, musicians, etc. This is a common competitive feature of most temple festivals in Kerala today. A representative example is the famous Trichur Puram in which three major temples in the city compete. The grand finale, with thirty matched tuskers in full panoply, held at the Vatakkunathan temple, is the largest in the immediate area. There is no prize, simply the renown attached to having been the very best that year. There is even an annual competition at the festival between two fireworks manufacturers.

The addition of these far more expensive elements has

necessitated a new arrangement for fund raising. A committee for each of the three processions is convened, made up of prominent citizens of the concerned hamlet or village, local landlords and businessmen. They appoint by agreement a working committee. The members of the working committee are not only honored but obligated to raise as much money as possible through subscribed donations to defray the cost of the festival. The donations are recorded and a printed receipt is given to donors. In addition to small donations by villagers and larger ones from prominent wealthy persons, the costly services of the elephants are sometimes donated by owners, but more often the elephants are rented. The cost is about Rs. 100 per day for each elephant, but a "famous" elephant can bring up to Rs. 500. The *janmi* owning the land upon which the temple is situated is an important patron. In the case of Kozhimambarambu, it is the Manazhimana Nambutirippatu near Puducheri, a hamlet north of the village of Cheruthuruthi. This more modern system of fund raising is widely in use in the Trichur and Palghat areas.

The expansion of the program of events in the festival, and the participation of upper castes by collecting funds or managing the committee, reflect an element of civic pride and a degree of inter-caste participation in the modern sense which is fairly new. The old system, on the other hand, depended for success upon patronage exclusively along traditional lines.

At the 1969 festival, a five-hour evening concert displaying various forms of special percussion ensembles was arranged. Professional percussionists of renown were invited from the surrounding areas of Cherppalacheri, Vilineshi, Tiruvillamalai, and as far as Kollenkode, thirty miles away — a *tour de force* never attempted in the past.

The elaboration of the festival, and changes in patronage and economy, have altered the old basic *jajmani* form. The old political and social relationships implicit in the pattern are becoming more blurred. Evidently vestiges of quite ancient orders of precedence, no longer clearly understood historically, are incorporated into the fabric of the events and structure of the festival. The order of precedence in dates of festivals in minor shrines before the final culminating festival, and the appearance of representatives of each of the minor shrine areas at the last festival, indicate that much more can be learned about the traditional formal structures of sociopolitical as well as religious interrelationships in the larger geographic area.

In the modern transitional period there are movements toward a wider-based popular spectacle and away from traditional order patterns (for example, five days instead of twenty-one days of the *Ramayan Tolpava Kuttu*). Supporting subscription funds are going into more impersonal performances such as the orchestral elaboration and a final fireworks display just before dawn. Much less "attention" is paid to the oracles of the priests of Bhagavati. Animal sacrifice has virtually disappeared in Central Kerala. Today and arrack drinking, a traditional custom of the past among the low-caste participants, is not an obvious feature of the festival now at Cheruthuruthi, though it is still practiced at the Kodungalur Bharani festival. At present many more people of upper-caste families observe the daytime festival as spectators; this was considered "not done" previously unless one was involved with the organization of events, and then among upper-caste families only males were permitted to attend. Western-educated Malayalis are no longer "embarrassed" by the traditional folkways of these rural festivals, but are beginning to take a more sophisticated and objective interest in the social history and traditional art forms of the area. Conscious recognition of and pride in Kerala's folk traditions by the Kerala state government is a new development of the recent period. This has taken the form of state-sponsored programs of folk-ritual dance and drama in the larger cities and towns.

Despite the comparatively stable state of these ritual arts of the festival at present, the prospect of their change and eventual demise is ever present. The economic and social base is already shifting slowly. If the context is changed and the real socio-religious function seriously disturbed, it will be their end. Once these ritual art forms fall within the orbit of the "synthesizing machine" of the urban middle class, their value will be changed. No longer viable in their original functional setting for study or analysis as institutions of the past or passing tradition, they will have already become part of the new cinema culture of modernization. Their documentation still remains part of the precarious future.

Kerala Village Temple Festival